Secrets of Successful People

About the Author

Gary McGuire has been working in the field of human functioning and strategic life planning for over twenty years. He is a Ph.D. in behavioural science from the University of Minnesota. A professional psychologist, he runs a counseling center in Dallas, Texas.

Secrets of Successful People

Gary McGuire

Epitome Books
New Delhi

First published 2009

Published by

Epitome Books

B-65 Mansaram Park
Near Nawada Metro Station
New Delhi – 110 059

Phone: 011-2537 1324
Fax: +91-11-2537 1323

Email: info@epitomebooks.com
Web: www.epitomebooks.com

Cataloging in Publication Data–DK
Courtesy: D.K. Agencies (P) Ltd. docinfo@dkagencies.com

McGuire, Gary.
Secrets of Successful People / Gary McGuire

p. cm.

ISBN: 978-81-906579-3-8

1. Success. 2. Self-culture. I. Title.

DDC 158.1 22

Printed at Salasar Imaging Systems, Delhi-35

Preface

It is well said: "Success brings people together, and failure makes them orphans." It applies everywhere and in all circumstances. For example, in the competitive exams very few succeed and the remaining remain unsuccessful. People call the winners as "Lucky ones," and the losers are called "Unlucky lot." This is human nature.

But, we can say confidently that all men are equal by nature. God has given intelligence equally to all.

But success depends on how we use our intelligence. Success is not hereditary. Success is directly proportional to the hard labour put in by people.

Luck is described as: "Hard work is another name for luck. Leave nothing to chance," is a golden word to be adopted and followed by those who want success in their activities or programmes.

I would like to express my sincere thanks to the publishers for their continued interest in bringing out this book.

Gary McGuire

Contents

1

What it Takes to Succeed

It is true that people don't seem to care about one another anymore, that we seem to have lost our compassion for our fellow men. In the light of this, those who have a physical challenge must show to others their capabilities so that others can witness our desire to be considered "normal." A positive attitude helps a person realize that they should always focus their own capabilities, rather than dwell upon their personal challenges. Many physically-challenged people I have encountered often have bright, bubbly personalities because they want others to recognize them for who they are. Many of their personalities are very much stronger, their voices all the more dominating, and their enthusiasm for life all the more contagious.

Accepting a physical challenge requires a friendly personality, which often develops early in childhood. With this friendly personality comes an uplifting attitude that motivates anyone's spirit. To motivate others, first consider if the following applies to you: "I just want to be a good friend, that's all. You can call me a leader, but please do not call me a follower. I have been on that trail; it's so worn down that it's not useful to follow anymore. I'm forging a new one. So be willing to hold my hand, I will show you the way. It's a long journey, and it will take some time, but it can only begin through small steps."

So let's start with this: you have a physical challenge. Big deal! A disability is only apparent if the person allows it to be! You are not going to be a bodybuilder anytime soon. You are not going to be called a "stud" by any of your friends. You are not going to be able to walk normally. You are not going to get that dream job of yours. Well, let me tell you that there is one problem with you if you agree with these statements. It's your attitude about life, it's just too negative! Buddy, if you want to succeed in today's rough-and-tough world, a positive attitude is not only important, it's critical! A smile is what you will find on my face not just today, but all year long. A smile symbolizes a positive attitude. So let me see that smile of yours, it's an important first step on this journey.

Once you have that smile, you start to feel better about yourself! Wow! But the smile's presence seems to fall short of your expectations. Let me see if I can help you out here ... ahhh. Here is your problem! It's with your heart, it's not big enough! You know for sure that you would fail yourself personally if you don't open your heart. Open your eyes to the world and witness all the different cultures. The different people. The different lifestyles. The different clothes. And believe me, you will discover all these treasures wherever you go. All sorts of people have different treasures. All of them! Did you discover yours? Perhaps not. Perhaps not yet! And it all starts with you. No one can open your heart for you... you must do it yourself. And if you cannot open your heart, I must leave you behind. If you do, then we can succeed. And we can do it together.

So what's the next step on this journey? Well, do you have a dream? The fulfillment of dreams is only possible if you happen to be an over-achiever. I do not think you are ready for that, at least not yet! Dreams are not realized without effort, ambition, and drive. And we must transform these words into action. Roll up your sleeves. Be prepared to sweat. I am, and have been sweating for quite some time. It's not the physical kind of sweat, but it's more of a mental kind. You see, I am still continuing my education. And it's challenging for me. And I enjoy the challenge. So that would be your next step on this journey: you must accept the challenge to realize that dream of yours. And be willing to work hard to reach it.

While you are often working hard to achieve your long-range goals, you will have to consider that you will face frustrations along the way. But the key here is not to let these frustrations get to you; otherwise, you have failed in your efforts. As far as my own dream goes, my many earlier attempts to walk normally were met by numerous falls.

2

What is Hope?

Have you heard the above titled beautiful song by Leann Rimes, whose lyrics are by Mark D Sanders and Tia Sillers?

"Whenever one door closes, I hope one more opens. Promise me that you will give faith a fighting chance. And when you get the choice to sit it out or dance, I hope you dance."

I really hope you will dance and not sit it out. I hope you will, live each day and each year of your life to the fullest, so that you will have hope and look forward with confidence and back with no regrets.

With hope and optimism everything depends on you. Do not be afraid to be happy. Having hope gives you the strength to understand that absolute certainty never arrives.

Your best companion in life is your own hope. Keep your hope with you all the time. The ability to live with hope through everything in life is a great inspiration and provides strength and knowledge.

Hope is the most important healing force. Hope of recovery, hope of loving and being loved. Never say there is no hope. When there is no hope, there is no life. Better to say, "Where there is no hope, I will build it." With hope, your mental attitude and your personality will develop a better life and destiny.

With great hope you will face the future optimistically.

It's terribly important that we hang on to hope and never call a brownout a burnout. When there is a temporary overload on the emotional system, do not lose hope. Just rest, a new dawn will arrive.

I am talking about attitudes such as Hope, Optimism, and a Positive Outlook.

Perhaps we do not yet understand the human mind and body enough to provide answers why hope and optimism are so beneficial to us.

But they are!

What is HOPE?

Hope is the belief that you will be able to meet your goals and the expectation of good things. The desire for something good is the basis for believing that good will come. With hope one believes that all obstacles are challenges rather than dead ends.

Focusing on personal hope will help us to develop a more positive, goal-oriented thinking.

If you can believe it, you can achieve it.

The best medicine in the world is hope, a positive attitude and optimism.

In these days we really need more medical doctors who will prescribe hope and optimism as medicine. Optimists are healthy people because our health depends on our hope. Hope is a force with a powerful influence.

Discouragement, negativism and hopelessness will sap you of the power to act.

And people who don't act are like dead people.

We need to learn how to fight pessimism and bring more optimism and hope into our life.

We all suffer various trials in life, some of us more than others. Why do some people try and try again, whereas others seem to give up after relatively minor difficulties?

The way of thinking can make the difference.

If you have thoughts such as, "I am a total failure" or "I am of no use to anybody" you are putting a big "STOP" sign in front of you. No actions, no solutions, and no power lead to a lot of excuses.

Fight back your pessimism. Say to yourself, "I know my negative thoughts are destructive. I am going to fight them."

You are right, because your pessimistic thoughts are your overreactions. You are catastrophizing. Push aside negative thinking.

When you lose a job or money or an opportunity, you are losing a lot. But when you lose hope, you are losing everything.

With hope you can gain anything. Do not lose hope.

Hopelessness is a sickness that goes together with pessimism, depression, apathy, and anxiety.

Today many medical doctors believe in the value of hope as a therapy. "Hope is a powerful therapy," asserts Dr. W. Gifford. They know, for patients with hope and support survive longer and suffer less pain.

Consider a study on the role of optimism and pessimism in coronary heart disease.

A researcher comments, "Most of the evidence shows thinking positively is good for your health". This study provides some of the first hard medical evidence for this idea in the arena of cardiology.

Hope and optimism are crucial not just for health. Even longevity has been linked to optimism. When older people were exposed to fleeting messages linking the aging process with increased wisdom and experience, they were later found to walk with increased strength and energy.

The improvement was equivalent to the result of a 12 - week exercise program!

Can you believe that? I hope you will!

3

Your Life as a Mystery School

Mystery schools once existed throughout the ancient world - Greece, Egypt, India, China, South America. These spiritual centers provided a place where students could receive a mystical education by progressing through a series of spiritual trials and initiations. The goal was to provide seekers with the highest levels of spiritual realization - to understand the deep truths of existence, the cosmos, and human life. Initiates of these schools were credited with wisdom, as well as great magical and occult powers.

The main method of teaching the Mysteries was through myths - stories with deep mystical and psychological symbolism; for example, the Greek and Roman myths. In reality, these stories possessed two different levels. On the mundane level, the myths could be seen as simple entertaining tales with light moral undertones. For most people, this is how they would be received. These were the Outer Mysteries.

However, for those with eyes to see and ears to hear, there existed the Inner Mysteries.

Students of the Outer Mysteries would be carefully observed. Some would show signs of recognition - a clear ability to see beyond the superficial level of the stories to the more profound meaning. These few would then be selected for further initiation into the Inner Mysteries. They would serve under the tutorship of the Master (Hierophant) of the Mystery School and be taken to ever deeper levels of spiritual unfoldment.

The teachings were hard. The initiation ceremonies were dramatic and frightening - seemingly life and death situations where the student was exposed to his deepest fears and temptations. Perhaps the mythological stories would be enacted in the depths of a dark cave to the sound of loud gongs and frightening flashes of light. Frankly, nobody really knows. Initiates were sworn to strictest secrecy, even unto death, and these matters were never written down.

Thanks largely to the efforts of organized mainstream religion throughout history and the world, the Mystery Schools have mostly vanished on the physical plane. However, they still exist on the spiritual level. More excitingly, they can come alive right now for YOU in a personal way - through a profound study of your own unfolding life.

Prior to your birth, imagine that the spiritual part of you - known as the Higher Self - made some decisions. It determined precisely the lessons and experiences you needed to undergo in order to learn, grow and perfect yourself in all ways. It then chose exactly the right parents, and the right time and place for you to be born. Ever since your birth, it has been orchestrating ALL the events and people in your life to perfectly present you with all the challenges and lessons you most need in order to develop yourself. From this perspective, nothing happens in your life by chance. Everything has a meaning. There are NO accidents.

What is the goal of all this? What is the purpose of your life from this perspective? It is no less than to become a Spiritual Master over as many lifetimes as it takes!

THIS is the perspective of your life as a Mystery Story. The Master Teacher of the Mysteries is your Higher Self. Through the trials of ordinary life, -through perceiving the mythic dimensions of it - you are presented with the lessons you most need to learn in order to perfect yourself in all ways.

It is a theory which cannot be definitively proven. However, as the great mystical teacher, Paul Solomon, once said, life works far better and makes more sense if we assume it is true, even if it is not!

The Mystery School perspective is very similar to the way in which we regard dreams. Modern psychology postulates that every person, object and situation in our dreams has deep symbolic meaning. They are created by a part of our mind that understands and thinks only in symbols. The challenge is for our waking consciousness to then make sense of all these meaningful symbols.

This is EXACTLY the same situation that is presented with our waking lives from the Mystery School perspective. In a sense, as long as we participate in life unawares, we are still asleep. As soon as we realize and actively participate in the Mystery School lessons of our lives, the sleeper awakens to progressively greater levels of awareness.

If your life is a Mystery School, everything that happens to you is by design. There are NO accidents. Every person who enters your life, every situation whether joyous or tragic, every challenge you face, is there for a specific reason. From this viewpoint, you have to stop blaming your parents all the time for the way you turned out. After all, you chose them!

Like King Arthur, Perseus, or Odysseus, you are the hero of your own personal Mystery Mythology. The events and characters in your life are the colourful fabrics of which your story is woven.

People and circumstances that you perceive to be enemies and trials are in fact your greatest teachers. In the Mysteries, the initiators could appear to the student as demons or monsters - evil forces that had to be overcome before any further progress was even possible. These were in truth archetypal forces within the pupil's own psyche that needed to be wrestled with and brought under control before any further progress could be made.

Yet, once the lesson had been learned and the demon overcome, it reveals its true form—as an angel of light. As the Dalai Lama once said, we need to be grateful to people who mean us harm, for it is only through conflict that we can grow. From a Buddhist perspective, there is even more need for gratitude to enemies: they are actively harming themselves, incurring massive negative karma, specifically to benefit you! And they don't even know it!

How does this apply practically? Well, have you noticed that certain scenarios - work difficulties, relationship problems or whatever - keep cropping up again and again for you? The reason is that if you refuse to learn a lesson, it will simply repeat again later until you do. Please don't think that you can go on to the advanced lessons until you have mastered the simple ones.

It will not happen.

Wherever you go in all the world to escape a lesson, you take yourself with you! Thus, you can be sure that your Higher Self will simply orchestrate events to present the exact same lesson/challenge until you finally get the message.

Moreover, remember this. The Higher Self regards your body as perfectly expendable! After all, if you refuse to learn the lesson in this life, it can simply provide you with a new one and the same lesson can start over where it left off!

In summary, viewing your life as a Mystery School is immensely beneficial. It provides you with a powerful spiritual perspective. It makes sense and meaning out of all that happens to you, enormously increases your chances for growth, and helps you work towards a firm purpose that transcends yourself - the goal of becoming a Spiritual Master.

4

The Power of Awareness

Normally, personal growth has to be consistent by each and everyone in their daily routine. For many people, self improvement is an ongoing necessary process. By improving ourselves, we dramatically improve our outcomes and opportunities in our life.

Personal development is a path that takes us to the desired location where we want to meet our goal. It helps us improve our career, spirituality, emotional health, and every other aspects of our life. Basically, personal development is about making conscious decisions about everything that we do, the way we think and the way we respond to situations. It helps us to attain everything that we always dreamed of.

Here are a few steps on personal development which can be helpful:-

- One of the biggest steps toward personal development is a change of mindset. If you think that you can do better, you will. When you think positively, you will find that you put forth more effort into everything that you do, and you will have much better results. Everybody needs a strong support system and reinforcing positive feedback.
- Another important step towards personal development is to set obtainable goals. This is not to say that your dream is not obtainable. But if you constantly think about the goal

of being a millionaire with a successful family, you will feel pretty hopeless as that goal seems so far out of reach. Setting obtainable goals simply means that you set goals that lead to the ultimate goal.

For instance, when you decide that you need food in your refrigerator, it does not automatically appear. You must make a grocery list, go to the grocery store, shop for items, purchase them, bring them home, and put them in the fridge. Obtaining a large goal is much the same way. You will not get them overnight. It takes going through a series of steps, or smaller goals, to find your way.

- For some people, personal development is also a matter of moving beyond past failures and their bad luck to see what is possible in the future. Often the major obstacle would be the negative comments made by their own friends and family and it is difficult to overcome.

To overcome all these problems, Personal Development coaching was created especially to educate and motivate individuals who desired a positive vision for their life. These are called "Life Coaches" and the teachers embrace powerful strategies for self management and personal growth. There are different categories of life coaches. Each life coach has his/her own area of specialization and unique approach. Some teach how to change habits, while some embrace more spiritual design platforms. Personal development coaching can include anything from how to improve your relationships to overcoming public speaking. Weak areas that exist in your life can be strengthened by calling a life coach.

Not everybody needs a life coach, ascertaining whether or not you need one depends on your needs. If you just cannot work through the setbacks, or if you need to learn new behaviors, then you probably want to consider seeking out a life coach. Everybody is doing it, so never feel you have to struggle alone. You owe it to yourself to maximize your human potential. The first step to self improvement is acknowledging your weaknesses. The second step is to find the help you need. A life coach could be your saving grace.

5

Be Smart in Goal-Setting

A goal is having an objective already visualized in your mind. It is the end result or achievement for which an effort is directed.

Like a cab driver hailed by a passenger with a specific route or itinerary of stops in the performance of the passenger's work or duty, you are responsible for getting your passenger to his/her destination in proper state. You are the driver of your own motor vehicle or life. Likewise, you are responsible for your own decisions and actions to accomplish your goals in life.

How does the endeavor of reaching goals become achievable? It is simply through setting goals. But how does one set up goals? Setting up goals constitutes of a driver and a vehicle. You, yourself are the driver of your goal and the vehicle is the means of completing your specific goal.

There are certain directions in setting up for one's goals. An acronym is provided below which are definite ways to help you carry out your objectives:

1. Beginning. To start acting on your goals, you must "begin with an end in your mind."
2. Ending. Have a clear-cut picture of your goals in your mind. This way you become fully aware of what you really want to achieve.
3. Specific. Goals should be "specific, personal, and in present tense."

4. Measurable. You can define your own method of measuring your objectives or goals. This can be in the form of personal rewards for internally motivating yourself is a hard-earned habit and discipline as well.
5. Attainable. Attainability of goals is measured by the level of commitment towards achieving it. Ask yourself, "How willing are you to get it?" Are you the type who says, "I'll try", "I'll do my best" or "I'll do whatever it takes."
6. Realistic. What one accomplishes must make sense and is rewarding or relevant. "Are your goals realistic for you?"
7. Time-bound. Set a deadline to complete your goals within a finite time. Have a time-frame for your goals and be amazed of what you have attained.

Remember, "Be smart." Before I end this article let me share this wonderful quote, "Having a simple clearly defined goal can capture the imagination and inspire passion. It can cut through the fog like a beacon in the night."

What is a Goal? Goal (Noun)

The result or achievement toward which an effort is directed; aim; end. Every January, when you set resolutions, you truly intend to follow-up on them. It's likely that among your goals, you have both personal and professional targets you're aiming to accomplish throughout the year.

As a Business and Life Coach, this is also the time that many of my clients work hard to finish their Business Plans and set up their other business goals for the next twelve months. You probably do the same, and these goals may include things such as:

- Increasing sales.
- Enhanced employee relations.
- Better time management.
- Advance a new marketing plan.

Sometimes, you set goals that you think will be really easy, when in reality, they're not. Maybe you only have ten pounds to lose, and you figure that will be simple. Or perhaps you simply want to be home thirty minutes earlier each night - that should be a breeze, right? These goals don't seem hard, but it can be that lack of "bigness" that makes us underestimate the process. This can be the difference in whether we actually achieve the results we want or not.

So what are your goals? Is this going to be the year you really take time to set and go after those goals? If you need help figuring out what your goals are, my Business and Life Planning guide might be helpful to you. Are your goals too easy? Or do they seem too hard? What is that one goal you have for yourself in 2008? Let me know!

3 Steps to Achieving Your Goals

Every year people set out at the end of the year to make New Year resolutions. Unfortunately, only a few people ever stick to their resolutions. People don't have the commitment or accountability factor needed to maintain their resolutions. We all mean well, we have every intention of following through with the resolutions. A good example is the resolution to lose weight. It never fails, every January the gym is so crowded you can barely find room to exercise. Like clockwork, the gym attendance slacks off by the end of February if not before.

However, all is not lost. We just need to adjust our strategy. Forget about making resolutions. Set goals and become a goal-getter. Once you set your achievable goals and start achieving them; you will be an expert goal-getter. Here are three simple steps to setting and achieving your goals:

1. Decide what you would like to accomplish

Set your goals and do strategic visioning to see yourself accomplishing those goals. The goals should be aligned with your core values. You will be more successful at achieving your goals if they are aligned with your values. The goals should be specific and measurable. For example, you would like to write a book. The specific is writing a book. The measurable would be seeing the book completed. You should know your end steps. What will you be doing, saying or hearing to know that you have achieved your goal?

The goals should be achievable. This means, you should not have an impractical, impossible dream. For example, having a goal of a million dollars falling into your lap. That is not achievable by any stretch of imagination. You could start with small goals that are achievable to give yourself the track record of being able to achieve your goals. As time goes on your confidence increases and you keep striving higher until you reach your greatest goals.

The goals should be achievable in a specific time frame. You are not reaching for someday. Someday does not exist on the calendar, which means that you will never reach your goals. I am sure you have heard someone say, maybe one day I will be able to do that. Well, it will never happen unless that person put a time frame on it and work towards it.

2. Write it down

The goals must be taken out of your head. They must be written down so that they become tangible. Also, you are giving the universe notice of your order. Writing also cements the goal in your subconscious mind. Having the goals on paper gives you a visual to refer to everyday to keep them fresh in your mind. The more you see them and visualise them the more they become real to you. Before you know it you will be acting as if you already achieved those goals. Some people even advocate writing the goals down every day as part of your meditation. In addition to writing the words, you can also paste pictures of your goals on vision boards and in journals.

3. Do action steps

This is the most important step. You must take action in order to achieve your goals. Think about it. If you are seeking employment, do you sit at home and wait for the job to come to you. I don't think so. You send out your resume, you go on interviews and you do follow-up calls. Well, working on achieving your goals is no different. Look at your goals and decide what actions must be taken in order to achieve these goals. Let's go back to the example of writing a book. Some of the steps that you need to follow are: 1) decide on the topic

2) do research and

3) do an outline.

You should be doing at least one action step towards your goals each and every day. Each step will take you closer to your goals until you have achieved them.

It also helps if you are accountable to someone. So partner with an accountability buddy so that you can keep each other on track. Your goals are more effective if written in this manner: It is now March 31, 2008 and I am at Barnes and Noble doing a book signing for my book titled, *Golden Life Living for Real People.*

Take note that you are writing the goals in the present tense; that makes it more real to the subconscious mind and more believable. Note, that it is achievable; there is a specific goal and a specific time frame.

6

How Can I Improve My Self-Esteem?

Self-esteem is something almost anyone can use more of. Even the people who exude confidence on the exterior probably have nagging doubts in their heart of hearts—doubts that they carefully hide from those around them, but which gnaw at their souls. Doubt can be debilitating.

Luckily, anyone can take very practical steps to improve their self-esteem. Confidence in ourselves isn't something we're born with overnight (unless we're just cocky, in which case the confidence is probably ill-justified!). Anyone with a brain and a critical eye is bound to see what's wrong in their lives. But it's always constructive to remind yourself of what's right—and that, in any case, things can improve still more.

Below are just a few great pointers on how to increase the self-esteem.

Take stock of yourself.

Begin by asking yourself which areas of your life and personality need the most work. What changes would you be most proud of, and find most fulfilling? Compose a list of them—five, perhaps, or ten at the most (if you're really self-critical!). Rank them. Think about how you can go about improving each point.

Build yourself up.

Don't get discouraged, dwelling too much on the areas you want to improve. Remind yourself of the progress you've made thus far in life. Pat yourself on the back for having enough determination to try self-improvement in the first place. You're on the right track!

How will you get there?

It's not enough to decide where you want to go in terms of self-esteem; it's more important to ask how you're going to get there. Also, who can help get you there? Whom can you trust for help, and for counsel, and even for a shoulder to cry upon, if you have a temporary setback?

Counter-attack: Tired of suffering the blows of fate? Tired of feeling like the football of the gods? Go on the counter-attack! Take action! Formulate a battle-plan, and assert yourself. You can make things happen. You can dish it out too, instead of just absorbing the blows.

Spread the wealth: Self-esteem is something of incomparable value. At the same time, it's something you've got to give in order to get. The more you build up the people around you, the more that same enthusiasm and confidence will reflect back on you. Spread that sense of optimism and excitement to every member of your team.

Branch out: Extend your sphere of influence, and allow yourself to be influenced by interesting and stimulating new people, as you become a member of new organizations and interest groups. Find people who share your passions, and exchange ideas.

Engage in extra-curricular activities: Take up a new side project, something you'll enjoy. Make it something you'll find relaxing, and yet exhilarating at the same time. Something that will improve you and make you a more well-rounded person. Perhaps it'll be a hobby or club or recreational activity.

Never stop learning: Don't allow your thinking to stagnate. Join a class, on some topic you're interested in—even if it's something not directly connected with, say, your career, or your primary goal in life. As long as you're passionate about it, you'll benefit from this intellectual stimulation. Its positive effects on your main interests may surprise you.

Migrate to warmer climes: If you've got a bad case of the blahs, or are stricken with cabin fever, strike out for new territories. Exploring an undiscovered country can revive your outlook on life, and inspire you with new ideas and new influences. Take a vacation, or even consider making a permanent move, if you really need a fresh start.

Count your blessings: Never forget to remind yourself of how blessed and, ultimately, how happy you really are. Consider it as an added bonus if your dreams come true; if they don't, right away at least, you'll enjoy the challenge, at the very least.

7

How to Behave with Neighbors?

Man is a social being and he cannot live alone in this busy modern world.

From dawn to dusk, he has to interact with a large number of people with whom he comes across daily and has to work together with them either in the office or in other fields where he has to do his job.

At home he has to maintain a good relationship and rapport with his neighbors.

It is strange but true, many a time we actually don't know, who our neighbor is. Such is the situation often we face. With the help of these tips, we can a maintain cordial good co-ordeal relationship, especially with our neighbors and also with others.

1. First of all, take initiative and talk to your neighbor with a smiling face, (even if you're very busy), if you happened to see him face to face. Never wait thinking that your neighbor should take the initiative.
2. Never forget to invite your neighbors for the functions and for any other happy occasions, which might take place in your home of and on.
3. Arrange small get-together parties and invite your neighbors.

4. Move with them freely, but never try to take undue advantage by interfering in their personal affairs. Also do not get involved deeply in their matters.
5. But if they tell something to you, just listen to what they say and keep quiet. Otherwise, politely tell them, that you have no time.
6. Persons without any work or job never keep quiet, but go on spreading rumours and passing unnecessary comments against others. Never participate in such type of discussions.
7. Better to be calm in such type of situations.
8. Remember: "Speech is silver, but silence is golden."
9. If there are more than three or four families in your locality, maintain friendship with all of them, otherwise there are likely chances of developing groupism.
10. Even if you are having a thick and thin relationship with your neighbors, never visit their homes after 8 in the evening.
11. If any one of your neighbors is suffering from any ailment or is in any need, immediately offer your services and respond to their need immediately.

The golden rule is: "A friend in need is a friend indeed".

10. Never give free advices, which unnecessarily invite troubles. If they seek your help or advice, give your valuable opinion or advice to them.
11. If you have prepared a new recipe, do offer it to them and obtain their suggestions.
12. If you happened to visit a new place, and bought some novelties that were sold there, offer some of those novelties to your neighbors. Such gestures will endear you to your neighbors.

8

Role of Smile in Personality Development

A smile on your face is enough to change your surroundings. A smiling face is like sunshine. It is a wonderful feeling to be greeted by a complete stranger with a friendly smile. It is a nice feeling to smile and be smiled at. Smile does wonders in our real lives. A smile can set you free from bonds like sorrows and worries. A smiling face plays a vital role in the enhancement of one's personality.

The smiles of Leonardo Da Vinci's painting Monalisa brings cheer to every heart and also for that matter, the smile of a small brings the same sensation in our hearts. A pure smile can generate positive vibes not only in your home but also at your workplace (office).

When you smile, it will be returned, definitely. A smile prolongs our life-expectancy.

A smile costs us little energy and brings us happiness. A serious looking face needs all the 64 muscles in the face to be activated, whereas a smile needs only 13 muscles in the face to be activated.

If you go into history, a smile did such a glorious thing that it saved a person from death.

During the Spanish Civil War, Antoine de Saint Exupery was captured and kept in a prison cell. It was clear without any shadow of doubt that he would be put to death the next day by the authorities. Saint Exupery wanted to smoke, as he had no matches, he requested the jailer if he had matches.

While lighting the cigarette, the jailer accidentally made eye contact with Saint Exupery who was smiling (without any reason). Even though the jailor tried to be stiff, the smile of the Saint Exupery drew the jailor into a conversation and he also laughed. What happened soon after was that the jailor helped the saint to escape from the prison and saved him from death.

Moreover, man is the only living being who can smile, in the whole creation of God, the Almighty. It is the gift given to humans by God. If you see any one without a smile, give one of yours.

Smile costs us nothing, but offers many dividends. So smile wholeheartedly and earn profits in real life.

But never forget the golden rule: "Laugh with a friend, but not laugh at a friend". Never hurt your friends with crude jokes and comments. Human life is a wonderful thing and make it happier with a little smile.

16 Tips for happiness in life

As per the observations and opinions of world famous persons and celebrities, the following tips are helpful in creating happiness in one's life.

1. Happiness is within us and is not found outside our body. We are solely responsible for our happiness and creating happiness in us. No other person can keep us in a happy mood forever.
2. Happiness begins in us, as soon as we observe and appreciate goodness in others. The main thing is, take care to keep around you only the optimistic persons as far as possible.

3. Never try to change others, as you may not succeed and unnecessarily you may invite trouble. It is always safe to be ready to change yourself.
4. Cultivate the good habits which you like very much and they leave you in a happy mood. For example, listening to good music, reading books, and playing with children etc.
5. Always show keen interest in your family and in their wellbeing.
6. Always be ready to accept the things that may occur without our involvement. In life, there is every possibility of occurrence of unexpected events. Usually we don't know what is going to happen in the next moment.
7. Take it easy if any unwanted event occurs (as anybody can pass unnecessary comments against you). Don't react immediately to such type of comments.
8. Never become a prey to stress and strain, which might spoil your health and leave you worried. Keep away from jealousy, envy and anger, etc.
9. Develop a strong desire to accomplish great things in your life and work sincerely to achieve it. Develop an interest in social service, as service to human beings is the same as service to the God, the Almighty.
10. Do exercise for half an hour daily, which releases feel good hormones (endorphins) from the body. Brisk walking is the best form of exercise.
11. Always keep a smiling face and tell others to have a smiling face, as smiling is like sunshine for our body. Everyone likes to see a smiling face.
12. Love others as you love yourself. God is Love. So loving others is a divine quality which gives you plenty of happiness.

13. Listen to good music. Do yoga and meditation which relax your body.
14. Never indulge in harmful habits like –smoking, chewing tobacco and drinking alcohol, etc.
15. Take a good nutritious diet, containing vitamins, minerals, proteins, and fibres etc. Take one glass of grape juice daily, which contains more anti-oxidants (cancer-preventing substances) and prevents blood clotting and heart attacks.
16. Have faith in GOD—The Omnipresent, the Omnipotent, All Pervasive and the Superpower who is the creator and protector of this universe and who gives you bliss.

9

Twelve Do's and Don'ts to Get Respect from Others

Sometimes, even educated people behave in unnatural ways in petty matters and appear cheap in the eyes of others. To avoid such embarrassing situations, it is better to observe the following 12 do's and don'ts.

1. Never read the letters of even your closest relatives, friends, and family members like brothers/sisters. If you read their letters, they will thinks that you lack manners.
2. Never show interest in others peoples' personal matters and don't read their personal diaries.
3. Never see the SMSs in peoples' cellphones. Never peruse through the contents of other people's wallets.
4. Don't see their albums, unless they want/tell you to see them and do not pass comments about the album's nature and external appearance.
5. Switch off the cellphones or keep them in silent mode when you are attending official meetings, cultural programes and also during dinner parties in the presence of guests.
6. Whenever guests come over, open the door, invite them politely, and walk behind them (not before them) and make them seated comfortably.

7. Whenever you visit your friend's house, carry some fruits, sweets, biscuits or chocolates, etc. for the family.
8. Whenever you take help from others, express your gratitude by saying words like, "thanks," etc. They will form a good impression about you. Give tips to waiters in hotels or restaurants.
9. During parties or in functions take the food items along with the guests (not alone) and also it is good to serve each other and drink together. It is a good social behavior.
10. While taking coffee, tea or cool drinks in the office, always keep the files on your left side (not on the right side).
11. A simple smile on your face costs nothing but fetches big dividends.
12. Whenever anybody visits your home, usually they bring something for you and your children. Reciprocate in the same manner.

The golden word is: "Mannerisms makes a man, good manners make a good man".

"Give respect and take respect" is a good slogan and keep it in your mind, wherever you go and whatever your profession and position may be.

Ten virtues for success in life

Nobody is born efficient or inefficient. We need to follow the following ten requirements to achieve success in life and develop a good personality.

Ten requirements to lead a happy and successful life:

1. First things first:

Before commencing or undertaking any work or project, we have to think twice and should know about the things to be done first. For example, we may have to mobilize sufficient finances and able to secure skilled manpower, etc.

2. Be proactive:

One must be highly active in one's daily activities and be moving.

"A stagnant water becomes dirty and emits bad odour, whereas flowing water is clean and fresh".

So moving or being active is nature's phenomena and it doesn't like laziness. The same applies to us also, if we want to succeed in life. Hence be prompt in your attempts.

3. Think win and certainly you will win:

Positive motivation is a good sign to get success. You know pretty well that "faith moves mountains." There is always hope in positive thinking. Any work well started is equal to work half done. So, never despair and always dream about success and you will be crowned with success. But there should be no lacunae in our efforts.

4. Aim to overcome the obstacles:

Certain problems might crop up unexpectedly, viz. scarcity of resources, shortage of men, lack of unity, powerful rivals, ill-health, etc. We should not get disappointed when countered by such problems. Only weaklings give up at this stage. The capable ones analyze the problems carefully, plan accordingly and take suitable steps to get over them.

5. Find out new methods (angles):

When things are moving at a normal pace in an organization, there is scope for improvement. Therefore, one should take to innovative methods to improve further the quality and speed of work. That prompts them to invent new angles of operation in this direction. Fix the time-limits for each and every type of work, which are being undertaken in your organization or at your place of work. One should keep pace with the changing times.

6. Seek advices and suggestions:

One should continue seeking the suggestions and advices from his colleagues and other experienced persons in that field. Otherwise progress comes to a standstill. Whatever may be your place in the hierarchy of your organization, success should always be your motto.

7. Have the confidence:

Confidence is nothing but trust, which provides the tryst for transactions. Confidence should emanate from within, on the self first and on others next. Be trustworthy not only in your family but also in the organization where you work. For to obtain confidence, one has to work hard, to prove his worthiness and dependability. Be straight forward, keep the promises you have made and behave with justice towards others, and in turn they will bring good reputation and trustworthiness to you from others.

Remember always "trustworthiness is the backbone for anybody to work in any organization". A liar can't thrive.

8. Take timely decisions:

Taking a proper decision and also at the proper time is a crucial factor and one should not postpone it. If need be, one may consult either elders or superiors, analyze the issue and take appropriate decisions.

9. Sharpen the saw:

Always be in touch with the latest information and sharpen your brain with up-to-date knowledge. As the saw needs periodical sharpening to cut better, our brain needs periodical feeding with the latest information available in that particular field, where you are working.

Nowadays, we find heavy competition in every field. We should also not lag behind in obtaining the latest information.

10. Find alternatives:

If there are two or more alternatives for your decision, proceed in a systematic way. Devote considerable time and make a list of the alternatives available along with their merits and demerits and the likely consequences and repercussions. If necessary, take the help of experts in that field. Then discuss with them in detail and implement the right alternative method which helps in improving the quality of the work and also the image of the organization.

10

Secrets of Successful People

It is well said: "Success brings people together, and failure makes them orphans." It applies everywhere and to all the circumstances. For example, in competitive exams, very few succeed. People call the winners as "lucky fellows," while the losers are called "unlucky people". This is human nature.

But, we can say confidently that all men are equal by nature. God has given intelligence equally to all.

Success, however, depends on how we use our intelligence. Success is not hereditary. Success is directly proportional to the hard work put in.

Luck is described as: "Hard work is another name for luck. Leave nothing to chance," a golden word to be adopted and followed by those who want success in their activities or programes.

Another golden word is like this, as told by a great person:

"Genius is nothing but 1% percent inspiration and 99% perspiration".

But one must keep it in mind that success is not so easy as it appears. Ask any successful person how he succeeded in his endeavour, and immediately he will reveal the troubles he faced before he came out successfully.

The winners were relentlessly working hard, while we were sleeping. They read day and nights and sacrificed number of their happy moments and also their luxuries. They also never forgot the hardships they underwent during their childhood.

But one should not get discouraged at the time of failure. Most of the successful persons were also at one time failures.

Remember that, "Failure is the stepping stone to success". Never stop even if you fail one or two times in your attempts. Pursue it until you obtain the fruits of success i.e., the goals in your life. Usually the failed one say the cause of their failure is their fate and God did not help, and hence they are unlucky. They should not forget the fact that the cause of failure lies in them as they did not make sincere attempts.

So try to rectify if there are any defects in you. Be always calm and cool and think in clear terms how to complete the project or programe which you have undertaken.

The following are some of the differences between winners and losers:

Winners:

1. Usually, they control their anger, if at all it arises and they never allow their feelings to dominate them.
2. They have plenty of self-confidence, steadfastness and are always honest.
3. They have the capability to do hard work.
4. They develop friendship with very few persons and that too only with their well- wishers.
5. They study everything with a concept- based mentality.

Losers:

1. Usually, they are hasty and have a confused mentality.

   As the phrase goes:' Haste is waste."
2. They make friendship with a large number of people, but most of them are in the habit of spoiling their friends.

3. They are devoid of courage, but are full of inferiority complex, cowardice and scold others for their faults.
4. They do not take competitive exams, do not very seriously and read the books at that time only.

Suggestions:

1. Attempt anything sincerely, (otherwise leave it).
2. Some sort of commitment should be on your part, as God helps only those who help themselves.
3. Take inspiration by reading the life-histories of great persons and keep them as your role-models.

Then certainly success favours the losers, the next time.

Art of Living- How to live happily?

Sri Ravi Shankar has explained how to live happily and purposefully in this world.

1. He says firmly that we must have an aim in life.
2. Stream is different from flood. In a stream, the water flows in a systematic way. Whereas in floods, the water flows as it likes.

   In the same manner, the energy present in us should flow like water in the river, as it has got certain direction, otherwise, nothing but confusion prevails. Nowadays, the majority of the people's condition is without any specific direction, just like a ship without a rudder.
3. When you are in a happy mood, so much life-energy is accumulated inside the body. Never allow it to stagnate there and rot. It should flow freely.
4. Life runs with commitment only. Every small or big thing in our life, goes with certain commitment. For example: 1. A family runs on commitment, 2. A mother is committed to the child and a child in turn to the parents. 3. A wife is

committed to her husband and vice versa, 4. A student takes admission in a school or college with a commitment.

5. Commitment is highly essential to make this life energy to flow into the right directions.
6. We feel delighted when we take troubles for the sake of our family members. We never take it as labor or hardship, but we feel it "as our responsibility". It is nothing but our commitment to our family.
7. If you extend this same kind of commitment beyond your family limits to your neighbours also you will get plenty of joy.
8. Similarly creativity is also important and it springs up when you are relaxed. Unless you renounce all the work you have done that whole day, you cannot at the night and have sound sleep.
9. Millions of people in this world are struggling or frustrated, because they are not creative. So take out some time for yourself to spend it in meditation, which in turn improves the quality of your life and helps you live peacefully in this busy world.
10. Unless you know the art of living, you cannot live your life, you cannot enjoy the happy moments in your life and also bear the sadness in the life.
11. You wish always that you should not get troubles or face hardships, and life should go easily.You will never think of future as you are confident that future is bright. But that is not the real life and is almost equal to a stone, which is motionless and is aimless.
12. The adage is "life is not a bed of roses but full of thorns". Life is a combination of light and darkness, joy and grief and good luck and bad luck which follow each other in a sequence. We cannot avoid and deny them but have to

invite and bear them happily. But they are with us temporarily and leave us in a happy situation.

13. Spend silent moments for a certain period of time and in silence you will get the benefit of prayer, which brings faith or self-confidence.

11

How to Overcome Inferiority Complex?

Almost 25 to 30% of people suffer from inferiority complex the main reason being their hesitance to take a step fearing other people's opinion. They often feel shy and dejected, degrade themselves and do not enjoy their rights even at the minimum level.

Behavior of people with inferiority complex:

1. They hesitate to speak fearing others might misunderstand them, even though they have conversational skills.
2. They get their hair cut neatly, but still feel shy and often wear a hat to cover their heads, thinking that others might laugh at them.
3. They take it easy even when the newly acquainted persons also dare to crack jokes against them (they don't protest).
4. They calmly eat the dish supplied in a hotel even if it is stale, because they think that waiter might feel offended if they make any adverse comments against the preparation.
5. They eat beyond their limits and suffer from stomach upsets whenever they go out for any dinner under obligation.
6. They lend their important books, articles, etc. to friends for few days under obligation and become tense, until they are returned.
7. They fall an easy prey to realtors and fake financial institutions, become members and burn their fingers.

8. They drink (alcohol) and eat junk foods in parties, much against their wish, out of obligation.
9. They go out to stand even near a lavatory being unable to withstand smell of smoking from a co-passenger in a railway compartment, instead of openly objecting to the smoking.
10. They hesitate to wear new dresses and shoes fearing that others might find them gaudy and make unnecessary comments.
11. They often get angry with family members, if they are asked to do a particular thing or to meet a certain person, as they are lazy and wish to be left alone.

We can quote many more examples. It was reported by psychologists that people of the above cited mentalities must have been pampered by their mothers and put to regimentation by their fathers, while they were young.

For example, parents often to suggest, "do this or do that, don't wear this dress or that colored suit," etc. Thus they lose their individuality and general thinking power and become habituated to depend upon others, even after marriage.

How to overcome Inferiority Complex?

- First of all have to develop a strong determination, to change their above mentality.
- Initially, they require a little initiative. They should be daring and should give up their inhibition.
- They should repeatedly remind themselves that they need not be afraid of anybody.
- They should develop positive thinking and try to express their views, even if they do not like anything.
- Everyone is unique in this world, so one should have his own individuality.

So let us start to lead a new way of life, from this moment onwards, keeping all inhibitions aside.

Causes of Fear – How to overcome it?

The following four things are common for all living beings:

1. Food: for living and survival.
2. Sleep: to recoup the body energy (as sleep provides rest to the body).
3. Sex: It is a biological need and it serves many purposes, like:
   - Calms up the excited sensory organs,
   - Removes the feeling of loneliness,
   - Helps control blood pressure,
   - Brings pleasure to the mind and body
4. Fear: What for?

All the above are found in all living beings, yet man worries about each. However, fulfilling the fast three things leaves one satisfied..

But in case of fear, the situation is different and it always accompanies us. So let us discuss about it and clear the doubts.

Even infants (children below 1 year of age) suddenly wake up from the sleep and show feelings of disturbance and excitement. That means, since our birth, the fear gives some sort of discomfort to us, with or without any cause.

The usual causes for the fear-complex are:

- Many fall prey to diseases by indulging in irregular food habits and other immoral activities.
- The rich spend sleepless-nights worrying about, how to save their huge amounts of money.

- People with name and fame in the society may think that one day their name may be tarnished, unless they behave carefully.
- Rulers are afraid of their enemies.
- Beautiful women and handsome men worry about their old age.
- The good and the noble people are afraid of bad and rowdy elements.
- Every living being worries about the inevitable death-feeling.

But is there any place on this earth to live safely and without fear?

How to overcome fear?

First of all one must know that what we are seeing and enjoying in this word are ephemeral (temporary) and they disappear from our sight one day. So we should develop detachment and be less inclined towards them.

We should also realize that which is eternal and truthful is nothing but God and once we realize this fact, automatically the feeling of "this is mine and this is I" goes out of our mind and we will be free from "fear". Otherwise the fear cycle goes on and there will be no mental peace to us.

Our role, as long as we live in this world is just like a trustee. Moreover, we are ambassadors of God, in this world. Everything here belongs to God.

The golden rule is: "Where there is detachment, there is no fear." Everything moves around depending on "attachment and detachment."

12

Tips for Happy and Successful Life

Each and everyone wishes to lead a successful life in his world, including yourself. We must know at least some factors that influence success.

Whatever you are, you are unique. You can certainly make a significant mark. You must wake up and take up the challenge. You will definitely come up in life.

We usually say that a certain person, who was insignificant earlier, is now earning millions and another person who had been very poor before, later on got educated with other's charity and has now become famous. May be they are very lucky people. Let them be so.

The golden word is: "Hard work is another name for luck. Leave nothing to chance".

Whatever be your status to start with, you must work hard sincerely and should become a great person, so that not only your family, the village/town but the country also feels proud of you as the great son of the soil. So be prepared and rest assured.

How to lead a happy and successful life?

1. Be modest, face the dangers with valor.
2. Anger should be replaced by endurance. Lead a chaste life.
3. Never bother about the past (impossible to change it), instead learning a lesson from the past and not commit the same mistakes are the essential qualities of a wise man.

4. Know your strengths: These are the plus points and some of them are given below:
   a. You have good health and are able to get sound sleep every night
   b. You have the tenacity of the purpose
   c. You are well educated and have the intention to acquire further knowledge in your field/profession
   d. You have conversational skills
   e. You are indifferent to criticism by others
   f. You are very pragmatic and not a mere day–dreamer
   g. You have a good family background
   h. You have the leadership qualities
   i. You are ready to work anywhere and can maintain good relationship with the public.
5. Know your weaknesses (if you have got any) also and try to overcome them:

Following are some of the weaknesses normally present in many persons:

1. Laziness
2. Unable to express your views clearly and people fail to understand you properly
3. Not able to control your anger
4. You feel jealous if others are successful
5. Finding fault with each and every person
6. You feel that you are not physically that attractive
7. Having the tendency of being partial towards your community people
8. You feel upset, if others criticize you
9. Not able to get rid of bad company of friends, etc.

Remember you have to do careful introspection to correctly identify your weaknesses and sincerely try to remove them, either by meditation or by counselling from experts.

Laughing - Tips and advice

Laugh is a boon given to man by God. But we are not utilizing it properly.

A child laughs 400 times in a day. The teenager and an adult laughs 17 times in a day. See the difference. It clearly shows that laughing gradually declines as age advances.

Stress is the main cause for lack of laughter. It is not good to be affected by stress. So laugh as often as you can.

Laughing tips:

1. Begin each morning with a laugh.
2. Stand before the mirror and wish yourself with a laughing face.
3. Laughing gives:
    1. Courage
    2. New energy
    3. Self-confidence
    4. Relaxion to the nerves

REMEMBER: Smile is fragile. Suppose when you are in a happy mood and suddenly you receive a phone call. The smile on your face disappears. But how many days would you like to live with such changing moods?

Get rid of these bad feelings. Always think positively. Be confident of yourselves.

If anybody passes a comment on you, never put a sorrow figure in front of him, as it gives pleasure to him. So you should be bold and be happy. Never give such an opportunity to others.

Laugh as frequently as you can.

Take this firm decision: Come what may, I am going to smile today and be happy forever.

13

How to Behave with Superiors in Office?

Your method of working in office is also a part of your behavior. Bad behavior by any one member can spoil the office environment. That's why group discussion, communication skills and working in a team are playing vital roles in getting good jobs. Your good behavior with superiors in an office will enhance your personality and you can command respect from juniors. Officers may have different personalities but we should apply smart tactics in dealing with superiors with difficult personality.

1. It is not a good idea to discuss your personal matters with the higher officials. Avoid taking advice or opinion of your superiors to solve your personal problems. Their advice or suggestions may not suit you and also sometimes you have to obey and act as per their advice, under duress which may be not conducive to the situation and may bring further trouble to you.
2. Never discuss with your seniors about your money or property matters and also about your debts. It is better that they don't know about matters that trouble you.
3. Keep away from the rumours in your office. Also, never discuss them with your officer.

4. Try to solve the problems or the doubts regarding the work in office matters, which you might have with your colleagues by discussing with them. If not possible, bring them to the notice of the officer and the officer in turn will settle the matters in group meetings.
5. Do your duty sincerely and dedicatedly, so that you need not say sorry to your officer often.
6. Keep yourself away from the quarrels or misunderstandings that may arise among the staff members.
7. Never promise to perform those tasks which are beyond your capacity. You may end up inviting trouble tarnishing the good name earned by you in your office.
8. If you have any physical or psychological problems, inform your superior officer and discuss it with him without any hesitation. Otherwise, it would hamper your work indirectly and the officer may develop a wrong impression about your working capacity. That is why it is better that you make it known to them, as sincerity always pays.
9. As your officer is an experienced person, observe him carefully and also his way of discharging duties. It not only benefits you but also helps you in handling the office matters.

"Obedience is the secret of success" and it does wonders in your life.

By knowing how to talk and also how to behave, depending upon the place and time, we can safely avoid and be away from so many problems, in our daily life.

Anger: causes, problems and management

Anger is the most common personality disorder that spoils relationships in everyday life.

Why do we get angry?

1. Thinking that the other persons' status and their thinking power are below your level and dignity.
2. Your ego is hurt when others disagree with you. You feel people have been disrespectful to you.
3. Your stubborn attitude expects others to fulfil your demands under all situation.
4. Your authoritative mentality leaves you with a appearance when dealing with others.
5. Habituated to controlling everybody and everything.
6. Having an inferiority complex attitude.
7. Being under the misconception that by exhibiting anger, it is easy to keep others well under your control or command.

Bad effects or problems due to anger:

1. Anger causes physical and mental troubles like,
   - Headache, hyper- acidity, pain in the neck region,
   - Lack of concentration in doing any work/studies, etc.
2. Your friend would show disinterest in speaking to you.
3. You feel too much stress.
4. You rarely laugh with your relatives/friends and your relationship with them gets spoiled.
5. People talk something before you and exactly the opposite is talked behind you.
6. Your moods are not under your control, that is, you don't know when you get angry or when you are in normal condition.
7. Nobody dares to give any valuable suggestion to you, as you think that what you know is the only correct thing.
8. After some days, you begin to get angry upon yourself and also develop inferiority complex.

9. You develop insecurity and begin to lose confidence in others.
10. First of all you get angry upon others and afterwards you begin to repent like that and the same situation will be repeated by you.

How to control or avoid the anger:

1. Read the biographies of famous persons (at least one or two persons) in the world and of those people who conquered anger.
2. Examine yourself and find out the causes of anger and write them on paper.
3. When you get angry, think about one humorous scene in a cinema, your anger will vanish in no time.
4. Count to at least fifty when you get angry and anger will leave you.
5. Ask yourself, "What I am going to achieve by exhibiting this anger?"
6. Change your way of thinking and be positive in your attitude and be patient and everything will be alright in the days to come.

The golden rule is: "No anger—no worry," but only happiness always surrounding you. Also keep it in mind that, "Somebody brings happiness wherever they go and somebody brings happiness whenever they go."

Same famous quotations on anger are:

1. "Your anger is your enemy."
2. "Anger is temporary madness."
3. "Anger is just one letter short of danger."

14

Ten Tips to Manage Stress

Stress is nothing but excessive reaction of the body to certain incidents which we face in our day-to-day life. Physiologically, excess of adrenaline secretion take place in our body and it has got abnormal negative effects, not only on our thinking, but also on our health.

Effects of stress on our health:

1. We take more food than is necessary, to appease our mind.
2. Indirectly it leads to overweight and further to obesity, which in turn leads to diseases like diabetes, hypertension and heart ailments, etc.
3. There is every chance of developing vitamin deficiency in the stress situations.

How to deal with stress?

These are ten simple ways to get relief from a stressful life.

1. Exercise regularly. This keeps the particular individual in a happy and active mood throughout the day. Treadmill exercise removes stress from the body through sweat and it is more useful in winter season.
2. Spend at least some time in the morning sun. It is a good stress reliever.
3. Spend as much time as possible among your favorite friends. This sort of personal relationship brings immeasurable joy and frees you from stress.

4. Take a hot-water bath, which removes the heaviness in the head.
5. Inhale and exhale deeply as it helps the body take in more oxygen which in turn helps the body to withstand the stress and strain.
6. Relax for twenty to thirty minutes whenever you are stressed.
7. Read a book which you like a lot, which acts as an inspiration and enhances your capacity to withstand the stress and strain.
8. Open up with people you like and adore most and keep them as your role-models.
9. Recap the achievements which you have attained till date, by your tireless hard-work and immense faith in your capacity. They will certainly provide you relief.
10. Have good food habits and preferably take a highly nutritious diet, containing more minerals and vitamins, etc. Avoid junk foods and eat only fresh vegetables and fruits.

Keep faith in God and take life as it comes. Work hard and leave the rest to God. He will take care of you.

Ten qualities of a successful leader

Everybody wishes to become a leader in life. Certainly, we have to welcome and appreciate his ambition. But by mere wish, one cannot become a leader. One should attain these leadership skills to become a good leader either in your personal or work life.

Ten leadership qualities:

1. BE DECISIVE:

He should be in a position to make timely decisions himself, depending upon the situation, without depending on others.

2. PRAISE SINCERELY:

He likes to praise other people's work and also encourages them further to improve their skills.

3. GIVE FEEDBACK:

He keeps the information channels open and allows them to flow in all ways, so that others (including his colleagues and employees) are in touch with the latest knowledge.

4. TEAM WORK

He should be in a position to join the staff to complete work at any stage and should not insist that certain tasks are below his dignity.

5. TAKE THE RESPONSIBILITY:

He takes responsibility for any untoward incident that occurs in the organization. He never passes the buck to others. He also knows pretty well, how to reprimand or fire the staff, if any serious irregularities are committed by them.

6. COMMUNICATE DIRECTLY:

If he wants to tell anything to his team he speaks directly to them and rarely opts for paperwork (for communication).

7. BE CREDIBLE AND CONSISTENT:

The leader is always credible and also firm in his approach, regarding any dealing with others. He never behaves unpredictably.

8. ENCOURAGE THE TALENT:

He likes to promote the talented persons among his staff members, to move responsible positions in the administration. He never assumes the notion that there is better talent elsewhere.

9. DISPLAY A POSITIVE APPROACH:

He thinks positively and also acts to improve the performance of the organization. He leaves no stone unturned and also tries to inculcate positive thinking among his subordinates.

10. HONEST AND HOLY:

A leader should be honest in his activities, as honesty always pays. At the same time, he must be like a holy person, without giving scope for impure thoughts and acts.

Remember the golden word as told by Napoleon (France), one of the world's greatest leaders.

"A leader is a dealer in hope."

15

Causes of Depression

Many of us suffer from depression, at same time in our life, which may be in varying intensity—from mild to serious types. Depression is nothing but losing interest or enthusiasm in life. There are so many causes or reasons for this type of mental agony.

Suicide- causes:

1. When a person loses his property in business.
2. When one is rejected or cheated by his or her lover.
3. When a person is suffering from a dreadful diseases like- cancer, HIV/AIDS, etc.
4. When a person is not able to secure a rank in the competitive test, thereby not able to get a job, or fails in the exam.
5. When one is neglected by his or her family members, including children.
6. When one problem is burdened with additional problems.
7. When a person with bodily disorder is jeered at by the people around.
8. When one is subjected to meaningless phobias or anxieties, etc.
9. When others, in the past, committed suicide under similar circumstances.

10. Often many women develop depression after giving birth to a child (during postpartum period), due to imbalances in levels of progesterone and estrogen hormones.
11. When he or she is suffering from psychiatric problems sexual disorders.
12. When a dear one panes away..
13. When reprimanded by a higher official without any valid reason.
14. When a person lacks a nutritious or balanced diet.
15. Occasionally, normal menstrual cycle aggravates depression, if already present in a woman.
16. Depression runs in some families as a hereditary/genetic trait.
17. Staying alone in cities and not showing interest in getting married also causes depression, especially in the youth, nowadays.

Signs and symptoms of suicide mentality:

Suicide-tendency is more common in women, (may be due to the fact that they are soft by nature) when compared to men. Moreover most of the males take many things in life very lightly.

1. Spend sleepless nights, thinking constantly.
2. Show no interest in food.
3. Either talk too much or keep absolute silence.
4. Write lengthy letters to people and never post them.
5. Keep away from friends or relatives, whom they like very much.
6. Often speak philosophically.
7. Show lack of interest in the activities dearer to them earlier.
8. Give away their valuable articles in charity.

9. Collect different types of tablets and store them discreetly.
10. Show lack of self-confidence and show displeasure and dismay.
11. Are always of the opinion that their life is a waste.

Management of the case (patient):

1. As far as possible, he should not be left alone.
2. He has to take a balanced diet, even if he is not having sufficient appetite.
3. It is well and good, if the depressed person shared his feelings with his close friends.
4. Exercise is good for them, as it releases endorphins which elate the mood of the patient. Walking is a suitable exercise for such people.
5. He may be under the false impression that depression is incurable, but the family members or friends have to enlighten him about the available latest treatment.
6. He should be taken to a psychiatrist for proper counselling and special treatment with antidepressant drugs. It is good to keep the patient under a psychiatrist's care for a certain period of time.

How to avoid depression and suicidal tendencies

Secretions, serotonin and nor-epinephrine, are neuro-transmitters, which carry sensual signals through the nerves in the brain. If there is a drop in their level in the brain, the person goes into depression.

Usually, every person feels depressed -that is natural and also beneficial to humans.

But every person must make auto–suggestions and try to correct them, if he had done any mistakes in the past. Automatically, he is relieved from depression. It is normally done by many.

Depression may be caused by:

1. Loss in business
2. Loss of friends
3. Failure in examinations etc.

In such cases, depression may be severe and the person remains continuously in that condition and is not able to recover himself. He leads a solitary life.

In lonely conditions, he never takes food properly and may fall prey to drugs and alcohol.

Ultimately he comes to the conclusion that "committing suicide is the only solution for his troubles".

Remedy: His family members or his friends must carefully observe the depressed person and must take him to a psychiatrist without loss of time for counselling and treatments with drugs. There are good numbers of drugs available for the treatment of depression.

16

Causes of Failures

It is said, failure is the stepping stone to success. However, every one is afraid of failures.

Characteristics of failed people:

1. They cannot execute their plans successfully.
2. They do not agree to analyze the negative points present in them.
3. They try to conceal the facts and try to deceive others morally.
4. They neither think of new thoughts nor wish to venture into new things. They like to adhere to old thoughts only—whether they are good or bad.
5. Obedience and dedication are not found in their dictionary.
6. They run behind in continuing further human relations.
7. They don't have any estimation and don't like to utilize their intelligence and energies.
8. They often say luck does not favor them, or their time is not good. It indicates that they do not sincerely attempt to do anything.
9. They are afraid of the word "failure."
10. They have a low self-confidence.
11. They hate to do hard work.

12. They are stubborn and are of the opinion that whatever they think is correct (even though it is wrong).
13. They have a butterfly mentality i.e. not fixed type. They go along with the wind.
14. They won't take any trouble to achieve the target.
15. Success and failure are the two sides of the coin. The failed people always see the negative side only. They do not like to turn the coin to see the other side that is success.
16. Success is not as easy as you think. The life histories of successful people show that they had suffered so many hardships to overcome the failure.

Five difficult things to follow in Life

Five Personality Development Tips:

If you follow these five simple but difficult tasks in life, you can achieve success by impressing others with your great character.

1. Keeping the secrets to yourself:

We feel some sort of uneasiness or distension in our stomach as long as the secrets are in you. Once you reveal them to others you feel so happy.

2. Always telling the truth:

Imagine how difficult it is to be honest and truthful. To lie is human nature even for silly things.

3. Keeping calm:

Thoughts follow. One who controls himself can control others.

4. Confessing mistakes:

It is very difficult to confer a mistake in front of others that I have done this mistake. One's egoism prevents one from doing so. We attribute the causes to others. So, confession requires great courage.

5. Promises should be kept:

It is very easy to promises make. It is very difficult to keep one's promises as it requires courage and belief in truth. Truth is God.

Seven common mistakes in our personality

1. The delusion: The individual's advancement should be made by crushing down the others. But it is a wrong notion.
2. Worrying unnecessarily: The tendency to worry unnecessarily about the things that can't be changed or corrected. We can't set the dog's tail straight.
3. Unnecessary arguments: Insisting that a thing is impossible because we ourselves cannot accomplish it. Nothing is impossible in this world.
4. Short sighted look: Refusing to set aside trivial things, so that important things may be accomplished.
5. Mentality of "I know everything:" They are of the habit of neglecting development and refinement of the mind and not acquiring the habit of reading and studying.
6. Compelling other to act: Attempting to compel others to do those things which they do not like to do.
7. Interfering in others affairs: It is a bad habit to put our fingers in other people's personal affairs, without their formal request.

If you wish for success in life, you need:

1. Perseverance—your bosom friend.
2. Experience—your wise counsel.
3. Caution—your elder brother.
4. Hope—your guardian genius.

To err is human; to correct is divine.

17

Eight Causes for Unhappiness in Life

Why are some people always unhappy while others face the same problems with a smile on their face. Cicero, a famous philosopher and statesman of yesteryears (2000B.C) belonging to Italy (Rome), enumerated the following causes for unhappiness, which holds well even today.

Eight weaknesses in the personality of unhappy people:

1. A dominating mentality: which may or may not be a human inborn trait.
2. Unnecessarily worrying about the things or situations which one can't change.
3. Inaccurate estimation of one's strengths and weaknesses which might result in heavy losses in ones professional or personal life.
4. Giving importance and evincing keen interest in petty things, which may be of no use to them in any way.
5. Never trying sincerely to improve ones mental power and not becoming mature.
6. Living under the impression that once views are only genuine and factual and expect others also to accept their beliefs.
7. Egoism—"I know everything and I need not need other's advice". Ultimately such type of personalities will land in darkness and troubles.

8. Getting involved in agreements. Such people think that "arguing always pays and meekness is weakness."

But what is the remedy? The surest and simplest way is: apply commonsense, depending upon the situations. But the pitiable thing is, as quoted by a noble personality- "commonsense is uncommon with the common people."

Unhappiness leads to depression and is a major cause for heart diseases. Unhappiness increases stress in daily life and it leads to lifestyle diseases.

Try to identify the weaknesses in you, by thoroughly examining yourself and sincerely rectifying them.

Always keep in mind others' welfare and also wish others to live like you. Ultimately you will find happiness within your reach, without any shadow of doubt.

So have no more tensions and no more worries not only in your lives but also in this world.

Silence role in personality development

Silence is the element in which great things fashion themselves. The bad effects of sound pollution on our health are deafness, loss of concentration, anxiety and tension.

Here we are mainly concerned about loss of concentration, which is highly essential to achieve anything in our life. Nowadays we are living in a society or world which is full of speed and busy with hectic activities.

We are totally forgetting that golden quotation: "Haste is waste."

To overcome this confused and puzzled situation, we need plenty of relaxation and mental peace, which can be attained by practicing "Absolute silence."

Steps to be followed to attain the silence:

1. Make it a habit of spending at least half an hour alone. During that half an hour period-
   i. Never talk to anybody,
   ii. Don't read or write anything,
   iii. Don't sit in front of TV and also not listen to radio programmes,
   iv. Try to control your thoughts.
2. Sit calmly or lie-down on the bed.

That means your brain or mind should be in "neutral gear" position. In the beginning, you feel that you are almost in hell, as human mind behaves just like monkey. But remember one thing that you are preparing to fight a war, which is against yourself only.

This war is on—laziness, ignorance, stupidity and carelessness, etc, which are present in you. Silence is the beginning stage in this war.

Observe the sea, which is calm and quiet and at the same time full of enthusiasm. Positive mentality helps us, to be like the sea. With the help of that knowledge, which is obtained during the silence, try to know ourselves. We can overcome these difficulties very easily and also our abilities will be increased manyfold.

Quote: Silence is a great doctor, a great guide and it is also the way to lead us to self-bliss.

18

What Makes You Happy

The magnitude of gratitude

Someone once asked, "What makes you happy?"

"What makes you unhappy?" came the reply. After all, if we are grateful for what we are, do, and have, how can we be unhappy? Such is the magnitude of gratitude. Our happiness hinges on it. The importance of gratitude, appreciation, or thankfulness never escaped the attention of the great philosophers. Marcus T. Cicero (106-43 BCE), for example, said, "Gratitude is not only the greatest of virtues, but the parent of all the others."

How about you? Are you grateful for all your blessings? Of course, we are grateful for the unexpected, pleasant surprises. For instance, if we were to win a lottery, inherit a fortune, get an unexpected bonus or raise, we would be brimming with thankfulness.

But what about the blessings we live with daily. Aren't we so used to them that we take them for granted? Here are some examples of good fortune that we may forget to be grateful for: food, shelter, clothing; the country we live in; opportunities to work, play, and study; the miracle of life; the misfortunes we have avoided; the diversity and spice of life; good health; our gifts and talents; our achievements; freedom of speech; the kindness, encouragement, and help we receive from others; the technology that makes life more pleasant (air-conditioning, appliances, computers); the ability to create our destiny with the power of choice; art, music, dance, poetry, and beauty; our friends, family, and pets.

Even our memories can be a source of great joy, for as Amelia C. Welby (1819-1852) wrote, "As the dew to the blossom, the bud to the bee; as the scent to the rose, are those memories to me." And what about nature; shouldn't it also be a great source of gratitude? Here's how Anne Morrow Lindbergh (1906-2001) answers to that question, "One can get just as much exultation in losing oneself in a little thing as in a big thing. It is nice to think how one can be recklessly lost in a daisy."

The point I was trying to make in the above two paragraphs was nicely summarized by Gilbert K. Chesterton (1874-1936) in one sentence: "When it comes to life the critical thing is whether you take things for granted or take them with gratitude."

But wait, there's yet another category of events and circumstances that we often neglect to be thankful for, and that's the difficulties we struggle with and the obstacles we have to overcome. For they are what make us stronger.

At this point, let me expand on what I suggested in my opening remarks; mainly, our happiness depends on an attitude of gratitude. Look at it this way, when we live with a grateful heart, we live without whining or complaining. In other words, we're happy. Or as Marianne Williamson has expressed it, "Joy is what happens to us when we allow ourselves to recognize how good things really are."

Despite the many handicaps she had to endure, Helen Keller (1880-1968) was grateful. Certainly you and I can do the same. Here is what she said, "So much has been given to me; I have no time to ponder over that which has been denied." That's what happy people do. They focus on what they have, not on what they lack. They do so for good reason, for as Epicurus (c. 341-270 BCE) taught, "Do not spoil (the pleasure of) what you have by desiring what you have not; but remember that what you now have was once among the things you only hoped for."

If you would be rich, be grateful, for gratitude is riches and complaining is poverty. Rather than complain about what you lack, be grateful for what you have. Charles Dickens (1812 ~ 1870) agrees, for he wrote, "Reflect upon your present blessings, of which every man has plenty; not on your past misfortunes, of which all men have some."

The next time you feel like complaining, write down your complaint and then change it into something you are grateful for. Do this often enough and you will develop the skill to always see the positive side in every situation. For an example of what I mean, take a look at this popular piece, taken from the Internet and titled, I AM THANKFUL:

I AM THANKFUL

For the wife who says it's hot dogs tonight, because she is home with me, and not out with someone else.

For the husband who is on the sofa being a couch potato, because he is home with me and not out at the bars.

For the teenager who is complaining about doing dishes, because it means she is home, not on the streets.

For the taxes I pay,

because it means I am employed.

For the mess to clean after a party,

because it means I have been surrounded by friends.

For the clothes that fit a little too snug, because it means I have enough to eat.

For my shadow that watches me work,

because it means I am out in the sunshine.

For a lawn that needs mowing, windows that need cleaning, and gutters that need fixing, because it means I have a home.

For all the complaining I hear about the government, because it means we have freedom of speech.

For the parking spot I find at the far end of the parking lot, because it means I am capable of walking and I have been blessed with transportation.

For my huge heating bill,

because it means I am warm.

For the lady behind me in church who sings off key, because it means I can hear.

For the pile of laundry and ironing,

because it means I have clothes to wear.

For the weariness and aching muscles at the end of the day, because it means I have been capable of working hard.

For the alarm that goes off in the early morning hours, because it means I am alive!

19

Using Time Wisely

Finding time to live?

An aerial view of most cities would reveal swarms of people frantically racing about. Everyone is in a hurry. If you stop someone and ask how they are, they will reply, "Busy. Very busy." They certainly are active, but often their actions are misdirected. They seem to be busy for the sake of being busy. They are involved in the business of being busy. Disheveled and unorganized, they are too busy to get organized. They are so busy mopping the floor, they have no time to turn off the faucet.

They pay a high price for their endless flurry of activity. At the end of the day, or before, they are stressed out. Instead of a life of serenity, they lead lives of frustration, resentment, and anger. Because they are too busy to have time for anything important, they feel empty. They feel as though they are plodding through a meaningless existence.

Also, because they have forgotten that people are more important than paperwork, their relationships suffer. They are worried about losing time, but not about losing their potential. They work hard for the growth of the company, but ignore their self-growth. The toll of their busyness is also the loss of excellence, for they abandon the practice of doing few things well for that of doing many things poorly. The speed at which they work causes errors and drains them of the energy that is needed to cope with problems.

Self-educated and author of eleven books, Eric Hoffer (1902 ~ 1983), had this to say, "We are warned not to waste time, but we are brought up to waste our lives." The cult of busyness is destroying our spirit. The problem, by the way, is not new. You see, the Chinese Character for BUSY is at least 2,000 years old. And the character is composed of two parts: the left side, which means SPIRIT (heart), and the right side, which means DEATH or DESTRUCTION. So, it was clear in the minds of the ancient Chinese that excessive busyness destroys our spirit.

How do we fight against the assassination of our spirit? By taking time to collect our thoughts. If we are to move from impulsive action to directed action, we need to take the time to plan, marshal our resources, and build our enthusiasm. If we are to go from "I'm busy" to "I'm productive," we must are our time to focus on what is important and then take purposeful action.

Our spirit is a creative force that has the power to bring about our dreams. But it needs quiet time to study our options, analyze obstacles, and build a road map to success. If we allow ourselves to get ensnared in a cyclone of busyness, the ember of our spirit's dream will be blown out. Many people are too busy worrying about what they've done to think about what they're doing. We have to reverse that trend by being aware of our actions, always thinking before we act, always reflecting on the results of our actions.

The question facing us is: How do we find the time to live? How do we disentangle ourselves from the web of busyness? Traditional approaches have been to turn to time management with the hope of learning how to squeeze extra hours out of the day. Assuming that I uncover another three hours a day to work with, how does that help me if I'm too exhausted to do anything else? So, the solution seems to lie in ENERGY management, not TIME management. To read about this fascinating idea and learn how to untap your energy with the Full Engagement Training System, get a copy of the New York Times best-seller, *The Power of Full Engagement* by Jim Loehr and Tony Schwartz (Free Press Paperbacks, 2003).

One of the best ways to save time is to do things right the first time. "Desire to have things done quickly prevents their being done properly." If you agree with that, you agree with the words of Confucius, who taught that in the 6th century BCE. There's something else you can do to regain control of your life, and it's something Confucius never thought of; mainly, turning off the TV.

Staying up late at night to 'relax' or get extra work done is self-defeating because you are denying your body the rest it needs to perform at top efficiency. Another mistake some make is refusing to say NO to the excessive expectations of family, friends, and coworkers. Sure, doing favours is fine, but when others do far less for you than you do for them, it places an unfair burden on you. You retain their friendship, but become your own enemy.

An excellent way to create more time is to perform several goals simultaneously. For example, when you take the family to the park for a game of volleyball, you are enjoying family time, calming the mind with recreation (re-creation), caring for your body with exercise, and recharging your spirit with the beauty of nature.

Another factor to consider is your interpretation of 'success.' Are you striving to HAVE more or BE more? I know a lawyer who sold his practice, moved to the country with his family, and opened an inn. He and his family have discovered they are getting far more from life, despite a far lower income. Do you really need a Hummer or will a Honda Civic do? The savings in the price of the car, insurance, maintenance, and gas means you don't have to work as hard. Is it a Hummer you want or happiness? Remember, even if you win the rat race, you remain a rat, trapped in the maze of busyness.

Both busyness and laziness lead to the same end, the neglect of important goals. Our task, then, is to treat time with the respect it deserves. After all, it is both a limited and a nonrenewable resource. Time is our lifeblood; it is destined to reap great benefits if we use it wisely. Of course, we cannot change overnight, making a 180-degree turn from a life of busyness to one of purposeful and carefully thought out action. But we can begin to take small steps today and bit by bit regain control of our lives.

If you are ever tempted to think that you don't have enough time, consider the poem of Purzil Crofe:

A busy man complained one day:

"I get no time!" "What's that you say?"

Cried out his friend, a lazy quiz;

"You have, sir, all the time there is.

There's plenty, too, and don't you doubt it --

We're never for an hour without it."

How can we complain that we don't have enough time when every hour of our lives contains sixty minutes? It's not time that we lack, but the willingness to make tough choices. Andrew du Frame tells it like it is, "There comes a time in a man's life when he has to make a choice. And there are only two things to choose. Get busy living or get busy dying." Which one will it be for you?

20

Watching Television

TV or not TV, that is the question. . .

Television is one of the greatest inventions of all time. For example, at 2:56 am Greenwich Mean Time on July 20, 1969, we were able to watch in our living room Neil A. Armstrong step out of the lunar module of the Apollo 11 spacecraft and haltingly walk on the surface of the moon. We were witnessing a milestone in the history of humanity. Such is the potential power of TV to inform, inspire, and unite.

Yet, in its current state, TV produces more problems than it offers blessings. The first problem—no matter how noble our intentions are to watch only worthwhile programes, once we start watching, it is all too easy to become ensnared in its almost hypnotic power to keep us watching regardless of the banality of the content.

I'm changing the subject for a moment, but there's a reason for it, so please bear with me. Now and then, an insect will find its way into my home. No matter how small it is, once it's spotted, my cat remains transfixed, and finally "attacks" the bug. My cat's behavior is due to what is called the "orienting response." That simply means that sudden movement grabs my cat's attention. We, too, have inherited this primitive response; the purpose of which is to alert us to the dangers of possible predators. Ever jump in fear because of a shadow or cringe in horror when something unidentifiable quickly moves across your path? They are examples of the orienting response.

The rapidly flickering, ever changing colors and shifting contrast of the TV screen seem to have the same effect. That is, TV captivates and transfixes us. So, before long, we are watching not for the content, but for the contrast, change, and captivating swirl of images. That is the danger. We may decide to catch a one-hour educational program, but find ourselves immobilized by TV's power and end up "watching" longer than we originally planned.

The behavior of many viewers supports the claim that we watch TV because of its power rather than for its content. The behavior I'm referring to is eating junk food and guzzling beer or pop while watching TV. What has this behavior got to do with the reason we watch TV? Well, you don't munch potato chips and drink beer while you're reading a book, do you? So, why is it done while watching TV? The answer is because TV is boring, and snacking helps to while the time away. By the way, according to a 1989 study by Larry Tucker at Brigham Young University, "Men who watch television three or more hours a day are twice as likely to be obese than men who watch for less than an hour."

TV also decreases one's attention span and weakens one's imagination. It weakens our attention span because we grow used to quick, short bursts of information. As a result, we grow impatient if it takes a while to make a point. TV weakens our imagination because everything is portrayed for us. All we have to do is sit back and observe someone else's imagination. Books are just the opposite. They increase our attention span and help to develop our imagination. We need to be more like Groucho Marx (1895 ~ 1977) who said, "I find television very educational. Every time someone switches it on I go into another room and read a good book."

The mesmerizing effect of TV brings us to an interesting paradox. You see, after a day's work, many like to regain some energy by first relaxing before the TV. But the "orienting response" and swirling TV images that I mentioned earlier result in information overload. This over stimulus of the brain sucks the energy right out of us. That's the paradox, we watch it with the hope of reenergizing, but get drained instead. Compare this with going to the gym for a workout after a tiring day at the office. Instead of growing more tired, we become energized. So, if you want more energy, far better to engage in some activity than to plop down in front of a TV.

Besides the hypnotic like effect it has, another major problem is the way it is used by those who own and run television stations and networks. TV is not made to entertain, educate, or enlighten us. It is made to sell products and services. To quote Dr. George Gerbner, Dean of the Annenburg School of Communications at the University of Pennsylvania, "Living with television means growing up in a world of about 22,000 commercials a year, 5,000 of them for food products, more than half of which are for low-nutrition sweets and snacks." TV, then, is the throbbing heart of the monster called consumerism. Women are forced to go to work and children see less and less of their parents, all so we can buy more and more of the stuff TV tells us is indispensable for happiness.

In the book *Abandoned in the Wasteland: Children, Television and the First Amendment* another paradox of TV is mentioned; mainly, "Every day, all across the United States, a parade of louts, losers and con-men whom most people would never allow in their homes enter anyway, through television." That brings us to the next issue, TV violence.

Doesn't the extraordinary amount of violence on TV have an adverse impact on society? Oh, I know intellectuals like to disagree with that point. For instance, Dick Cavett mocked the TV-violence debate by quipping, "There's so much comedy on television. Does that cause comedy in the streets?" His remark makes a nice sound bite, but shows little understanding of sociology. We are socialized. We are taught how to think and feel by the society, which consists of our parents, peers, schools, churches, role models, and, yes, TV. Of course it has an impact. To deny that is to say advertisers spend billions of dollars on TV ads that don't work. That's silly. TV ads influence us, and so does everything else that appears on TV.

TV creates great harm not only by its influence, but also by what it prevents. Marie Winn makes this point clear in her book *The Plug-In Drug*. She writes, "The primary danger of the television screen lies not so much in the behavior it produces - although there is danger there - as in the behavior it prevents: the talks, the games, the family festivities and arguments..." The three hours a day that the average person spends watching TV could be used in countless ways to grow. Want to master the art of digital imaging, write poetry, learn how to play a keyboard, study a foreign language, learn how to dance, or just get out and meet some interesting people? All that and more is possible simply by turning off the TV and using that time more wisely. There's much talk about life extension. People want to live longer. A 20-year-old man who watches TV three hours a day until the age of 70, could have extended his life six and a quarter years merely by turning off the TV. Shutting it off not only gets you to live longer, but to live BETTER.

21

What is Prudence?

Caution is a good risk to take.

Prudence is all about good judgment, weighing all the possibilities, considering the consequences of one's actions, thinking before one acts, being thoughtful, using common sense, doing what's best for oneself, using discretion, exercising caution, and conforming to reason and decency. It is the avoidance of thoughtless and reckless behavior. It is the ability to distinguish the difference between what is harmful and what is helpful and following the right course of action. Imagine how much misery would be eliminated if we all followed the dictum, "Look before you leap."

The Frenchman Pierre-Augustin Caron de Beaumarchais (1732-1799) was a musician, man of letters, publisher, diplomat, inventor, businessman, free-thinker, and master of controversy. In his composition, *The Barber of Seville,* Beaumarchais has one of the characters in the opera say, "I would rather worry without need than live without heed." Living without heed is reckless and, therefore, imprudent. But worrying without need is equally imprudent. You see, part of being prudent is being balanced; it is imprudent to be otherwise. Because of the need for balance, prudence may direct us to hold our tongue on one occasion and to speak up on another.

There are two types of risks, those with bad payoffs and those with good payoffs. A prudent person doesn't smoke because it is a health risk; it has a bad payoff. A poor man asking the rich woman he loves to marry him is risking rejection and humiliation. Yet, if she agrees, he will be rewarded with joy; his risk has a good payoff. So, prudent people avoid risks with poor payoffs, but have no problem taking risks that have good payoffs. After all, part of being prudent is valuing courage.

Some disasters are avoidable while others are unavoidable. The consequences of our actions are always unavoidable. But as long as they are governed by prudence, we will have nothing to fear. For as Shakespeare wrote, "Things done well and with care, exempt themselves from fear." Prudence, then, is a protective shield. And the absence of caution is more harmful than the absence of knowledge. Prudence is also the foundation of other virtues (good habits). For example, bravery without prudence easily becomes foolhardiness.

The political leader and writer Critias (c.460-403 BCE) was a relative of and respected by Plato. Critias recognized that people aren't born lucky, but create their own luck by leading prudent lives. That's why he wrote, "Fortune always fights on the side of the prudent." Despite Critias' praise of prudence, some argue that too much caution immobilizes one with fear and prevents progress. Such a belief, however, is based on a misunderstanding. Actually, it is impossible to be 'overly prudent' because to be so would be imprudent. So, the very idea of being excessively prudent is an oxymoron, or a contradiction of terms.

In the thirteenth century, the Persian poet Sadi (also written 'Saadi') wrote, "Learn from the misfortunes of others, so others may not learn from you." That certainly is good advice. Besides learning from the mistakes of others, prudent people also learn from the accomplishments of others. Every person we meet is an example, one to be followed or one to be avoided.

Let's consider some of the patterns of thinking shared by prudent people. First, they follow their inner voice and do what is right. The reward for their behavior is a life free of guilt, shame, regret, or stress. They also focus on the important issues because of their awareness of the brevity of life. They don't waste time; they live it, experience it, relish it, and use it. They also realize that what is prudent for one, may not be for another. So, they respect the uniqueness of others and allow them to express themselves differently. They are not only aware of the weaknesses of others, but of their own weaknesses. That's why they follow the advice of the German monk Thomas ã Kempis (1379-1471), who wrote, "Be not angry that you cannot make another what you wish them to be; since you cannot make yourself what you wish to be."

The prudent are so because of a conscious commitment they made. Whether they are aware of Caleb C. Colton (1780-1832) or not, they instinctively follow his suggestion: "Accustom yourself to submit on every occasion to a small present evil (inconvenience, effort, sacrifice), to obtain a greater good. This will give decision, tone, and energy to the mind, which, thus disciplined, will often reap victory from defeat, and honour from repulse." The prudent also instinctively heed the words of La Fontaine (1621-1695): "In everything consider the consequences."

The actions of the imprudent teach us what to avoid. They speak much and know little; spend much and have little; sleep much and do little; learn much and apply little. They also fear what will make them stronger and not what will make them weaker. When it comes to relationships, they often cut what could have been untied. They sever relationships that could have been mended, for they are intolerant and impatient.

Besides learning from the mistakes and good examples of others, we can learn from the wisdom of the ages, which is expressed in axioms, proverbs, sayings, maxims, precepts, mottos, aphorisms, dictums, and adages. In fact, let's begin at once by considering a few proverbs. Which of the following should you and I embrace?

First things first.
Forewarned is forearmed.
Eat to live and not live to eat.
Do as you would be done by.
Actions speak louder than words.
You can't tell a book by its cover.
Things are not always what they seem.
He who knows nothing, doubts nothing.

Knowledge is the mother of all virtues; all vice proceeds from ignorance.

A rainbow in the morning is a shepherd's warning; a rainbow at night is the shepherd's delight.

22

What's the Point of Life?

Take life as you find it, but don't leave it that way.

After work, the four members of the marketing team went to the pub for their weekly get-together. Unlike the past, today's subject was a heavy one. Instead of talking about sports, politics, or women, they broached the subject of LIFE. Casper started. "You know," he said, "life is nothing more than a sexually transmitted disease, and a terminal one at that."

"You're right," Xavier chimed in, "all life is, a substance that temporarily prevents our bodies from rotting." On a more benign note, Spencer yawned and said, "Life is something you do when you can't sleep."

While pushing the frame of his eyeglasses firmly on his nose, Errol added, "Here's what I think. A person who works hard and accomplishes a great deal meets the same fate as one that doesn't, for they both die. So, what's the point of it all if it all ends in death?"

Those who, like Errol, can't help wondering what the point of it all is are focusing on the wrong thing, death. For if you focus on life, the answer immediately becomes clear. The point of it all is to live a life of exuberance, joy, excitement, and wonder. The point of life is to experience the excitement of discovery, joy of achievement, and wonder of mystery. The point is to take delight in the surprises that constantly come our way.

Simply put, the point of life is to enjoy it; that is, to live IN JOY. Since we cannot give away what we do not have, it is important that we meet our own needs first. Ultimately, however, the reason for enjoying life is to make the lives of others enjoyable. For as George Eliot (pseudonym of Mary Ann Evans Cross, 1819-1880) wrote, "What do we live for; if it is not to make life less difficult to each other?"

Adam Lindsay Gordon (1833-1870) expressed similar sentiments in verse:

"Life is mostly froth and bubble,
Two things stand like stone,
Kindness in another's trouble,
Courage in your own."

The point of it all is to make a point, to have a reason for being, to be a point of light by making a difference. In other words, the purpose of life is to live a life of purpose. Usually, we don't have to waste time trying to discover our life purpose because it is not to be found, but to be created by us.

If your personal calling is not obvious to you, be still for a moment and ask your inner wisdom for guidance. Franz Kafka (1883-1924) explains: "Life's splendour forever lies in wait about each one of us in all its fullness, but veiled from view, deep down, invisible, far off. It is there, though, not hostile, not reluctant, not deaf. If you summon it by the right word, by its right name, it will come."

What's the point of being successful and having plenty to live on if one has nothing to live for? So, pick a cause. It is belief in something greater than you and enthusiasm in pursuing it that makes life worth living.

Some complain about the minor irritants and misfortunes that come their way. But so-called 'problems' are blessings for they provide the contrast that allows us to enjoy life. For example, Canadians love to escape from their harsh winters by visiting Florida and Hawaii. They find the contrast in weather delightful. So it is with the rest of life. The reason we enjoy the good times so much is because of the bad times. So, learn how to accept the bad with the good. Or, as Roger C. Anderson put it, "Accept that some days you're the pigeon, and some days you're the statue."

Others complain that life isn't fair, but that hardly is the case. After all, rich or poor, male or female, young or old, we all receive the same allotment of 86,400 seconds a day. That's fair isn't it? If some choose to use that time wisely and others choose to squander it, that's not the fault of life, is it? Also, what can be fairer than reaping what we sow?

Besides, as Lewis L Dunnington explains, "What life means to us is determined, not so much by what life brings to us as by the attitude we bring to life; not so much by what happens to us as by our reaction to what happens." Thomas L. Holdcroft shares an equally valid view, "Life is a grindstone. Whether it grinds us down or polishes us up depends on us."

Some believe in life after death, but what about life after birth? What's the point of life if you're not really living it? You probably agree with Philip Larkin (1922-1986) who wrote, "Life has a practice of living you, if you don't live it." So, get involved with life by doing and experiencing as much as possible. After all, not to engage with life is not to live at all. Isn't it better to die alive than to live dead?

Because of the brevity of life, the time to start living is now. Here are three quotes to forcefully bring home this message: 1. "For what is your life? It is even a vapour, that appeareth for a little time, and then vanisheth away (James 4:14). 2. "This life of separateness may be compared to a dream, a phantasm, a bubble, a shadow, a drop of dew, a flash of lightning." (Buddha, 568-488 BCE) 3. "When one subtracts from life infancy (which is vegetation), sleep, eating and swilling, buttoning and unbuttoning - how much remains of downright existence? The summer of a dormouse." (Lord Byron, 1788-1824)

Yes, life is like a taxi. Whether you're an active participant or not, the meter keeps ticking. But don't despair, for today you still have 100% of the remainder of your life left. You still have time to act. You still have time to make the right choice. And while we're on the subject of choices, remember that "There is a choice you have to make, In everything you do. And you must always keep in mind, The choice you make, makes you." (annymous)

So, don't take life for granted. Take it with gratitude. And leave it in better shape than you found it. Do you want to guarantee a successful life and peaceful death? Then follow the advice of Christian Fürchtegott Gellert (1715-1769) who wrote, "Live as you would have wished to live when you come to die."

23

What to do in Old Age

Don't just count your years, make your years count—Ernest Meyers

You may also be wondering if there are any signs of old age other than looking good and peaceful. Well, from what I've read, there are three signs of old age. The first is memory loss. Regrettably, I've forgotten the other two.... But not to worry, for as Leroy Satchel Paige (1906-1982) said, "Age is a question of mind over matter. If you don't mind, age don't matter."

1. KEEP BUSY. One of my favourite Japanese TV shows documents the lives of ordinary people 80-100+ years old. They are all in good health and enjoy life to the fullest. What do they all have in common? Well, they follow the examples of George Burns, Grandma Moses, and Bob Hope by leading active lives; they keep busy. They would rather wear out than rust out. Regardless of your age, engage in life fully. If you're not active, you're not living.
2. EXERCISE. In 1996, the U.S. Surgeon General reported that only about 17% of people over 65 are regularly active. Regular exercise, even if it is just walking, does more than keep you nimble and flexible. Exercise also reduces bodily toxins and maintains glandular health. It also tones the muscles, makes the heart stronger, and strengthens the bones. Stay active and you'll stay healthy.

3. EXERCISE THE BRAIN. Memory loss and a reduction in the capacity for learning may occur in some of the elderly. However, it is not because of their age as much as it is because of their failure to tax their brains. New brain cells grow throughout our lives, but unless we continue to use our mental faculties, the nerve cells will atrophy. It's simply a case of use them or lose them. Reading, studying, and learning new skills act as medicine and exercise for the brain. Working with computers and the latest technological marvels is another excellent way to stay mentally fit.
4. MINIMIZE STRESS. Stress is the enemy of physical health and mental acuity. It reduces the blood flow to the brain, reduces memory recall, and reduces learning ability. In the physical realm, stress is the leading cause of most diseases. Illness is aptly named "disease" because it is caused by being at dis-ease (stressed). To fight stress, take up yoga, taichi, or meditation. Long walks in the park, beautiful music, or painting also work wonders.
5. A HEALTHY DIET. The so called Mediterranean Diet (one high in fish, fruit and vegetables) forms a good basis. Additionally, seniors should make sure they get enough calcium and fiber in their diet as well.
6. DRINK PLENTY OF WATER. Dehydration is a common problem with the elderly. The recommendation is one ounce of water per kilo (2.2 pounds) of body weight. It's important to remember that alcohol, coffee, and soda pop do not count as water. On the contrary, as diuretics, their consumption doesn't add, but further reduces the amount of water in the body.

7. LAUGHTER. Laughter is a valuable aid to our well-being. It keeps us young by boosting our physical and psychological health.

In keeping with the spirit of laughter, here's a joke about the elderly:

Three old men are at the doctor's office for a memory test. The doctor says to the first man, "What is three times three?"

"274," answers the man.

The doctor says to the second man, "It's your turn. What is three times three?"

"Tuesday," replies the second man.

The doctor says to the third man, "Okay, your turn. What's three times three?"

"Nine," says the third man.

"That's great!" says the doctor. "How did you get that?"

"Simple," says the third man. "I subtracted 274 from Tuesday."

8. EMBRACE OLD AGE. When you embrace old age, you're embracing life. Don't run or hide from it. My wife's hair may no longer be black, but she is just as beautiful and a lot wiser. No wonder Marcus Annaeus Seneca (3 BCE-65 CE) said, "As for old age, embrace and love it. It abounds with pleasure if you know how to use it. The gradually declining years are among the sweetest in a man's life, and I maintain that, even when they have reached the extreme limit, they have their pleasure still."
9. HAVE SOMETHING TO LOOK FORWARD TO. By setting goals and cultivating hobbies, you'll always have something to look forward to. Your next vacation or art class, an

upcoming meeting with a friend, a visit to the theater, these can fill your life with enthusiasm and passion.

Here's how three others expressed the same idea: a) "While one finds company in himself and his pursuits, he cannot feel old, no matter what his years may be" (Amos Bronson Alcott, 1799-1888), b) "Keep on raging - to stop the aging." (Dale Carnegie, 1888-1955) "No one grows old by living, only by losing interest in living." (Marie Beynon Ray) In other words, we will remain young as long as we are planning for tomorrow.

10. WONDERMENT. We are miracles living in the midst of miracles. How is it possible to live without wonder and awe? And when we experience it, how is it possible not to be like children, not to be young at heart? Or as Sidonie Gabrielle Colette (1873-1954) wrote, "You must not pity me because my sixtieth year finds me still astonished. To be astonished is one of the surest ways of not growing old too quickly."
11. CHARACTER. "Nobody grows old by merely living a number of years. People grow old by deserting their ideals. Years may wrinkle the skin, but to give up wrinkles the soul. . . . You are as young as your faith, as old as your doubt; as young as your self-confidence, as old as your fear; as young as your hope, as old as your despair." (Douglas MacArthur, 1880-1964)
12. POSITIVE ATTITUDE. Pause and reflect on this quote from Samuel Ullman (1840-1924), "When the aerials are down, and your spirit is covered with snows of cynicism and the ice of pessimism, then you are grown old, even at twenty, but as long as your aerials are up, to catch the waves of optimism, there is hope you may die young at eighty."

13. REMAIN IN LOVE. Stay in love with life, friends, learning, hobbies, clubs. For as Benjamin Franklin (1706-1790) wrote, "Those who love deeply never grow old; they may die of old age, but they die young."

The renown geriatrician, Dr. Muriel R. Gillick wrote a good book on old age. It is called, *The Denial of Aging: Perpetual Youth, Eternal Life, and Other Dangerous Fantasies* and is available at Amazon.com.

I don't mind growing old because it's the only way I know of having a long life. I hope you feel the same way or better.

24

Why do we Exist?

We exist not for ourselves, but for one another.

Why do we exist? Not for ourselves, but for one another. This is what great thinkers have taught, whether it was Thomas Merton (more than 30 years ago) or Marcus Aurelius (over 2,000 years ago). However, you don't have to be a great thinker to realize this. Common sense is all that is necessary. After all, the fact that we are social animals is self-evident. We would not exist if it were not for the cooperation of two individuals (our parents). So, you see, we need one another.

Have you ever wondered why Canada geese fly in a "V" formation? Well, as each bird flaps its wings, it creates an uplift for the bird that follows. The uplift (somewhat like the slipstream of an airplane's propeller) allows the group of geese to fly 70% more efficiently than a lone goose. But isn't it more tiring for the lead bird(s)? Yes, it is, so they regularly change their positions during their flight. So, geese, too, do not exist for themselves, but for one another. By watching them, we can learn the importance of cooperation.

Not only in the animal world, but in the very building blocks of nature, we find teamwork, for protons, neutrons, and electrons join to form atoms. Atoms work together to create molecules. Molecules, in turn, make compounds, and so on up the chain. The web of existence seems to be based on cooperation. Or, as Preston Bradley wrote, "The world basically and fundamentally is constituted on the basis of harmony. Everything works in cooperation with something else." Our atoms, molecules, and genes are pulsating with cooperation; aware of it or not, it's part of our nature.

Cooperation, working together, or teamwork is the source of great power and creativity. In the past, businesses considered one another as rivals. Today, they form strategic alliances and benefit from the power that cooperation brings. In the arts, cooperation is the source of awe-inspiring beauty. Great works of music, such as Johann Sebastian Bach's, *Brandenburg Concerto*, for example, could come to life only because of the cooperation of artisans who made the musical instruments, music schools, composers, musicians, conductors, concert halls, patrons of the arts, and audiences.

Athletes epitomize the value of teamwork. That's why one said, "If you want to be incrementally better: Be competitive. If you want to be exponentially better: Be cooperative." Social clubs and business associations are other examples how members can gain power by working together. Also, governments form alliances and corporations merge to harvest the advantages of cooperation. And, of course, activists unite to bring about social or political change.

It's clear, then, we were made to cooperate and it is to our advantage to do so. If it's so clear, however, why is there more office politics than harmony in many workplaces? Why so many divorces? Why so much violence and crime? Why are we experiencing road rage? Perhaps we've forgotten about the benefits and value of cooperation. It may be time to refresh our memory, don't you think?

A young Buddhist initiate asked his mentor to describe hell. "Ah, hell," the monk said, "it is like a large banquet hall with countless rows of tables laden with sumptuous meals and delicious drinks." "But Teacher," the surprised initiate said, "I thought those in hell would suffer." "Oh, they do." answered the monk. "You see, there are four-foot long chopsticks permanently attached to their hands. Although they can pick up the food, the length of the chopsticks makes it impossible to reach their mouths."

"That's horrible. Teacher, tell me about heaven." the initiate pleaded. "Ah, heaven," the monk sighed, "it is like a large banquet hall with countless rows of tables laden with sumptuous meals and delicious drinks, and permanently attached to everyone's hands are four-foot long chopsticks." "But Teacher, isn't that the same as hell?" the initiate stuttered. "No," the monk replied, "the people are different. Although they cannot feed themselves, they feed each other!"

The point of the story is that we create our own suffering by refusing to cooperate with others. When we work together, we not only succeed, but we do so with a clear conscience. It is always better to succeed without stepping on others or stabbing them in the back.

A point to remember is that cooperation means more than merely working together. It means creating a win-win situation so that everyone benefits and there are no losers. Or, as Euripides wrote about 400 years before the birth of Christ, "Joint undertakings stand a better chance when they benefit both sides." When we approach cooperation in this way, we will be sure to experience the rewards.

The rewards are many, for as Charles Dudley said, "It is one of the beautiful compensations of this life that no one can sincerely try to help another without helping himself." There is more than help involved; there is also transformation. Carl Jung explained it as follows, "The meeting of two personalities is like the contact of two chemical substances. If there is any reaction, both are transformed." During this week, let's reflect on the power of cooperation, remembering that our actions not only impact those we work with and ourselves, but each act also helps to shape the universe.

25

Wise Words

The difference between a mean word and a kind word is the difference between lightning and a lightning bug.

The Roman statesman, Cato, the Elder (BCE 234-149), taught "Speech is the gift of all, but the thought of few." When was the last time you thought about the power of speech? When speaking, are you always aware that we use speech to inspire, strike fear, dissuade, persuade, console, hurt, disappoint, encourage, educate, censure, exchange ideas, vent feelings, pontificate, argue, thank, threaten, ridicule, criticize, cheer, sadden, curse, brag, comfort, insult, provoke, incite, or apologize.? Before you speak, do you remind yourself that our words can express understanding, hate, love, praise, appreciation, resentment, kindness, respect, rudeness, or wisdom? How do you apply the gift of speech? Do you use it to tell jokes, spread rumours, wrench tears, recite poetry, or instill hope?

Have you ever been hurt by the remarks of others? Many have. That's why Pontianus, who was crowned Pope on July 21, B.C. 230 and reigned until B.C. 235, wrote in his Second Epistle, "The stroke of the whip maketh marks in the flesh: but the stroke of the tongue breaketh the bones. Many have fallen by the edge of the sword: but not so many as have fallen by the tongue." That's a strong commentary about the pain words can cause. But words don't have to hurt. They can soothe, uplift, and give support.

Do you realize how much power your words have to make a difference in the lives of others? Let's think about this for a moment. Suppose you encouraged two people today, motivating each of them to encourage two others tomorrow. If the process continues everyday, 128 people will have benefited by the end of the week. If it continues for two weeks, there will be 16,384 beneficiaries. What if it lasted for three weeks? There would be more than TWO MILLION people benefiting from kind acts that you initiated! But let's be conservative and assume that at the end of three weeks "only" one-half of one percent of that number would benefit. If so, there would "merely" be 10,000 people better off because of your two acts of kindness. Imagine if you were kind to two different people every day! Can you begin to appreciate the enormous power you have to do good?

Of course, the reverse is also true. That is, each of our unkind acts spreads and multiplies just as quickly. Is there any wonder there is so much suffering? Isn't it obvious the world is in desperate need of our acts of kindness? Can we afford to let a single day pass without a kind word? Let's begin to make a difference today. Although we can improve the world in many ways with the gift of speech, for clarity's sake, let's focus on one issue: ENCOURAGEMENT.

Plants need water and kids need encouragement.

"Save lives; save kids." writes Celeste Holm, "We live by encouragement and die without it - slowly, sadly, angrily." The number of sad and angry children is rising. So is the rate of crime. To put the brakes on crime, we need to build more lives, not more detention centres and prisons. We build lives by nurturing our children. We must encourage them every step of the way, for they become what we encourage them to be, not what we nag them to be. As they struggle to become responsible, they are sure to stumble along the way. At such times, let's remember that a word of encouragement during a failure is worth more than an hour of praise after a success. If they engage in inappropriate behavior that requires a scolding or discipline, guide them gently. The purpose is not to instill fear, but to build confidence. As Johann Wolfgang Von Goethe wrote, "Correction does much, but encouragement does more. Encouragement after censure is as the sun after a shower."

When nurturing our children, we begin by accepting them as they are. After doing so, we then encourage them to become more than they are. William Arthur's words seem to describe how children may feel, "Flatter me, and I may not believe you. Criticize me, and I may not like you. Ignore me, and I may not forgive you. Encourage me, and I may not forget you." We are all standing on the shoulders of others. We have reached our present station in life because of the help and encouragement we received from others. The best way to return that favour is by picking up our children and placing them on our own shoulders. The best friends children can have are parents that constantly encourage, inspire, and guide them in becoming what they wish to be. The only thing a good parent will do behind their child's back is pat it. How shall we use our gift of speech? Wisely. After all, as Edward Thorndike explains, "Colours fade, temples crumble, empires fall, but wise words endure."

26

Worth the Wait

Life is 10% what you make it, 90% how you take it.

Your first problem is you don't know what your problem is. Your second problem is your attitude. And your third problem is you are living in the future, neglecting the present, and forgetting the past. Now, let's consider all three issues.

You think your problem is that life is unbearable because you have to continue in your boring job until January and stay in school until August next year. Your problem is not a boring job or tedious study, but the wrong attitude. You seem to think that as soon as you arrive in California, your life will be filled with excitement. But I suggest that before you change your address, you address your attitude. You see, if you don't work on changing it now, when you move to California you'll be bringing more than luggage; you'll also be bringing your attitudinal baggage. In other words, if you think life is terrible where you are, it will be terrible wherever you are because life is what you make of it.

Your priorities may be mixed up. You think your choice of job and place to live are important for your happiness, but those decisions are minor ones. The only important choice you have to make is your choice of attitude. Irving Berlin (1888 ~ 1989) expressed this idea well when he wrote, "Life is ten percent what you make it and ninety percent how you take it." This sentiment is also echoed by Preacher Charles Swindoll who wrote, "Words can never adequately convey the incredible impact of our attitudes toward life. The longer I live the more convinced I become that life is 10 percent what happens to us and 90 percent how we respond to it."

So, it is not your current position that counts, but your current disposition, for attitude is everything. Yes, if you wait a year, you'll be able to leave for California with $23,000, but remember, a man with $23,000 and a poor attitude is a poor man, and one with $250 and a good attitude is a rich man. So, set your priorities straight.

You are studying Graphic Design and Photography so you can launch a new exciting career. But how can studying what you love be tedious? Can it be you want the glamour without the work? What will happen after you start your new career and discover, it too entails work? Will you grow bored and change careers again? Didn't you once dream of becoming a Programmer Analyst? You succeeded in that goal, but now are bored and want to change direction. I'm not suggesting that you should abandon graphic design and photography. I'm merely suggesting that before you change careers and make a big move, you need to change your attitude.

What exactly do I mean by a good attitude? I mean that you take pride in yourself and resolve that no matter what you do, you will always do it to the best of your ability, and do it with pride. If you're a student, become the best student you possibly can. If you're a Programmer Analyst, take pride in your work and do your best. If we are always doing our best, how can we be bored or uninterested? Enthusiasm is a natural byproduct of a commitment to excellence. When you adopt a winning attitude, regardless of the job you decide to take, you will always be a winner. Change that attitude so you can stop whining and start winning. It's okay to change jobs, but change your attitude first.

Another characteristic of people with good attitudes is that they always look for (and find) the good. You are spending far too much time looking for what is 'bad' about your situation. It's time to change your focus by looking for the good, counting your blessings, and appreciating what you already have. If you cannot appreciate what you now have, what makes you think you will appreciate what you will have? Yet another attribute of positive thinkers is their empowering language. For example, instead of saying, "I HAVE TO stay with my current job," (which makes one feel like a victim), they would say, "I CHOOSE TO (or WANT TO) stay with my current job because I want to receive my retirement benefits." (This type of statement makes one feel in control of life.) As you develop a positive attitude, it will sustain you under all circumstances, and you will finally realize what happiness is all about.

Another mistake of yours is to live in the future, fantasizing about a better life. I'm not saying that you shouldn't set goals. Not at all. I don't want you to be like most people who spend more time on planning their vacation than on planning their lives. By all means, set goals and make plans. But once you have taken the necessary steps to reach your goals, return to the present. Don't drift into a dream world, allowing the present moment to slip by.

Spend less time silently dreaming and more time silently listening to your intuition for guidance on which path to follow. And take advantage of the potential power of the present moment. For at this moment, now, you have the power to choose, decide, and act. You can decide, for example, to change.

You can commit to doing your best, looking for the good, being grateful, and using empowering language. You can also decide to develop patience and self-discipline.

Additionally, don't dwell in the past, but learn from it. For we can't move ahead until we have learned from our mistakes. Finally, I suggest you pick up one copy each of Keith Harrell's *ATTITUDE IS EVERYTHING* (HarperBusiness, 2005) and his *ATTITUDE IS EVERYTHING WORKBOOK.*

"A great attitude does much more than turn on the lights in our worlds; it seems to magically connect us to all sorts of serendipitous opportunities that were somehow absent before the change." -- Earl Nightingale (1921-1989)

"Nothing can stop the man with the right mental attitude from achieving his goal; nothing on earth can help the man with the wrong mental attitude." -- Thomas Jefferson (1743-1826)

Two-minute ATTITUDE drill: TO EVERYONE: You can trust me. I'm committed to excellence. I care about you as a person.

EVERY DAY: Do good. Do your best. Treat others as you would be treated.

FOR TODAY: Nothing negative will escape my lips.

27

Writing Affirmations

Thought is the sculptor who can create the person you want to be—Henry David Thoreau.

Have you ever been hurt by what someone said? Have you ever been encouraged by what someone said? Of course, you have. Such is the power of words. They can uplift us or depress us. They can shape us, make us, or break us. The messages that were constantly repeated to us as children have become a part of us. They sink into our subconscious and automatically replay in our mind as self-talk.

If you were constantly praised, you grew up with confidence. If you were constantly criticized, you grew up feeling powerless. If you were like most of us, you grew up with some praise and some criticism, so you are only partially screwed up. Once you are aware of the causes of your self-doubts, fears, anger and other forms of self-limiting behavior, you can do something about it. What can you do? You can replace the negative messages running through your brain with positive ones.

These positive messages are called affirmations. And with constant repetition, they will penetrate our subconscious. Once there, they will form new beliefs, which result in new behavior. Should you be practicing affirmations? Whether you agree with the practice or not, you are already doing so. You are constantly talking to yourself. If those thoughts are positive and inspiring, great! Keep it up!

However, if you find negative thoughts flooding your mind and holding you back, it's time to take control. It's time to start affirming what you want in life and control your destiny. You can do this by creating and repeating your own affirmations. Now, let's move on to what you should know about the proper construction of affirmations. The more you adhere to the following principles, the more effective your affirmations will be.

1. How to compose affirmations

Focus on what you want, not on what you want to avoid. For example, if you want to stop smoking, don't say, "I want to stop smoking" because that would focus on the behavior you're trying to end. If you keep thinking about smoking, you'll feel like smoking! Instead, focus on what you want by saying, "I want to live a healthy lifestyle." Now the focus is on a positive, healthy behavior. Don't worry, once the message reaches your subconscious, it knows that it is necessary to stop smoking to achieve a healthy lifestyle, so it will automatically create the desire for you to quit.

Keep your affirmation brief. If you try to say too much, you lose focus. Zero in on one issue at a time. Once your affirmation begins to materialize (in about 3 weeks), you can move on to another issue with a new affirmation.

Use the present tense. Don't say, "I WILL grow confident" otherwise your subconscious will keep postponing your desire to "someday" in the future. Instead say, "I AM growing confident."

Be specific. Don't say, "I am losing weight." After all, your subconscious doesn't know how much you would like to lose, so it may stop after you lose one pound! Instead, say, "I am losing 15 pounds by October 31st, this year."

Use the 1st, 2nd, and 3rd Person. When you speak to yourself, you use the first person. For example, you may say, "I am ugly." But this thought was planted into your subconscious by people saying, "YOU are ugly." Also, at times, you heard others speaking about you: "TOM is ugly." Your subconscious is used to hearing the 1st, 2nd, and 3rd persons, so do the same with your affirmation. In other words, "I am handsome. YOU are handsome. TOM (if your name is Tom) is handsome."

2. Removing conflict

If I use the affirmation "I am confident," isn't it because I lack confidence? If that's the case, isn't the affirmation a lie? How can I believe a lie? There are five ways to reconcile this seeming conflict.

First, reword the affirmation so it is believable. For instance, instead of "I am confident," say, "I contain the seeds of confidence and courage and nurture them daily." Or, simply say, "Each day I grow more and more confident." The exact wording isn't important, just as long as it is believable to you.

Second, realize that your affirmation is not a statement of fact, but an announcement of your goal. It is not a fact, but the first step in manifesting your dream.

Third, use denial. Instead of merely stating, "I am confident," say, "I am never cowardly. I am always confident." If you only said "I am never cowardly," you would be focusing on negative behavior, but because it is immediately followed by, "I am always confident," it remains a positive statement. The denial announces to the subconscious that its present image of you as cowardly is false.

The fourth technique is powerful. Use two sheets of paper. On one sheet write your affirmation 20 to 30 times. Each time you write the affirmation, you immediately write the thoughts that come to mind on the second sheet. Keep repeating. Affirmation and response, affirmation and response. As you do so, you will find your responses slowing changing. For example, your thoughts may flow from, "I don't think this stuff works," to "I suppose it is possible," to "I guess if I religiously practice it, it will work after all," to "I want it to work. I know it will work. I'm going to keep practicing every day until it does work."

The fifth method is to change your affirmation into a question. So, instead of, "I am confident," say "What do I need to do to grow courageous?" or "How can I become courageous?" Your affirmation becomes a question, which results in your subconscious inspiring you with a plan of action.

3. Practicing your affirmation

Before beginning, relax and clear your mind. Decide what issue you want to work on or what goal you wish to accomplish. Then, create your affirmation. Next, practice writing your affirmation and responses between 20 and 30 times. Do this every night before going to sleep. The thoughts you experienced will carry on as you fall asleep, hastening the time it takes before your subconscious accepts the affirmation and changes your behavior. Do this every day for at least three weeks before moving on to a new affirmation. Keep a journal and record all the changes that are occurring because of your affirmations. This will keep you focused, strengthening and speeding up results. Persistence and repetition are the keys. Never skip a day. Make it part of your daily routine. Energize your affirmation with emotion. How will you feel after you achieve the desired results? Experience those feelings now by visualizing your success. This will energize your affirmation and help it to bear fruit.

4. Manifesting your affirmations

Don't just sit back, waiting for your affirmation to magically transform your life. Start making things happen today. Your actions and affirmations support and reinforce each other. When affirmations and action steps are practiced simultaneously, explosive power is released, and your success is assured. So, do both.

For example, if I'm very shy, I may use this affirmation: "I am no longer shy. I am comfortable speaking to others." However, while I'm practicing the affirmation, I take immediate action. It doesn't matter how small the steps are, as long as I take steps. So, whenever I see someone I would like to speak with, instead of ignoring them, I now say "Hi!" as I walk by. No need to stop.

As I keep repeating my affirmations and this small step, I will happily come to the realization that speaking to others may be easier than I imagined. Soon I will be ready to extend my "conversation" from a brief "Hi!" to a lengthier "Hello!" Again, there's no need to stop or wait for a reply (I'm shy, remember?). I'm just taking small steps, but I am making progress!

Before long, I will greet others with a "long" three-word sentence: "How are you?" When I'm up to four words ("Nice to see you!), someone will probably stop me and start a conversation. "Where are you off to?" they may ask. Without hesitation, I'll probably say something like, "I'm going to the library."

Wow! Miracle of miracles! I just had a conversation with someone I've been wanting to, but too shy to speak to. How did that happen? The answer is, of course, it happened because of the power released by using affirmations and action steps together. And what they are now doing for my shyness they will soon be doing for other areas of my life! An exciting thought isn't it?

5. Reinforcing your affirmations

The procedures outlined above are sufficient for reprogramming your mind; however, to hasten and strengthen your results, you can reinforce your affirmations by applying one or more of the following methods.

Make your own 10-minute tape. Make a tape of the affirmation you are working on. Vary the wording and use the 1st, 2nd, and 3rd person for each statement. Play the tape while you are working on another project, just relaxing, or going to sleep. You do not have to listen to it; just make sure that it is close enough to be audible. (It doesn't have to be loud.) Your affirmation will be reinforced as your subconscious perceives the recorded message.

Here is an example of a recorded message:

I am confident. You are confident. Ravi (your name) is confident.

I am (You are, Ravi is) no longer timid; I am (You are, Ravi is) always confident.

I am (You are, Ravi is) never timid; I am (You are, Ravi is) always confident.

I grow (You grow, Ravi grows) more and more confident every day.

Every day in every way, I grow (You grow, Ravi grows) increasingly confident. . . .

(Repeat often enough to make a ten minute tape.)

Mirror, mirror, on the wall.

You can write your affirmation on cards, and attach one to the bathroom mirror, place one on the top portion of your computer monitor's frame, and another in your wallet or purse, next to your money. Now every time you look at the mirror, face your computer, or reach for some money, you will see your affirmation. There is no need to consciously look at it, read it, or say it. Its mere presence will serve as a trigger to reinforce and further implant the message in your subconscious. You will soon think of other places where you can put cards, such as in your car. Also, instead of a bookmark, use an affirmation card to keep your place.

28

Writing Poetry

Pulsating poetry permeates passionate people.

What better way to express life's significance than by poetry? For like our heart, our planet, and our universe, it carries its message rhythmically. But our universe cannot only be heard, it can be seen as well. In fact, the sight of it is far more spectacular than its songs. The same can be said for poetry. Its rhythm is merely the background accompanying imposing imagery painted by words.

1. Although art, literature, and music may not be necessary for existence, they almost certainly are for life. For as French scientist and philosopher Gaston Bachelard (1884-1962) wrote, "To feel most beautifully alive means to be reading something beautiful, ready always to apprehend in the flow of language the sudden flash of poetry." You see, not to experience poetry is, in a sense, not to feel and be aware of life.
2. Consider for a moment, the many levels there are in enjoying music. You can enjoy it at home. Yet, you will enjoy it more in the concert hall. And you would enjoy it even more if you were a member of the orchestra in the concert hall, still more if you were the conductor of the orchestra, and most of all if you were the composer conducting the orchestra. So it is with poetry. You enjoy it

most when you are the composer or creator. So, poetry is worth writing for the sheer pleasure it will bring.

3. Poetry is magic, for it unveils and reveals the beauty in our surroundings and experiences. Here's how Jean Cocteau (1889-1963) describes it: "Such is the role of poetry. It unveils, in the strict sense of the word. It lays bare, under a light which shakes off torpor, the surprising things which surround us and which our senses record mechanically." Another magical aspect of poetry is it distills life, much as Haiku (Japanese poetry) distills the moment. So, as a poet, you will share insights, reveal hidden beauty, and illuminate others with your sparkling revelations. Poetry, then, is an opportunity for you to express the inexpressible.
4. As a poet, you will grow increasingly aware of your surroundings, relishing the moment. For you will "Take a commonplace, clean it and polish it, light it so that it produces the same effect of youth and freshness and originality and spontaneity as it did originally..." (Jean Cocteau). In a word, you will restore to life "what is lost in translation." (Robert Frost, 1874-1963)
5. Poetry is a venue for you to express your emotions. Just as when the stings of the Stradivarius are stroked, they resonate and fill the room with music, your poetry will cause your soul to resonate, filling the hearts of your readers with the melody of life. Your poetry will allow you to share, contribute, move, and inspire. What's more, you will learn that your poetry doesn't belong to you, but to those who need it.
6. Another reason to write is for the challenge. Writing poetry is no easy task, for as Carl Sandburg (1878-1967)

wrote, "Poetry is the journal of a sea animal living on land, wanting to fly in the sky."

7. Following the path of poetry leads to growing more attuned with your inner life. It allows you to discover your hidden resources and become your own best friend. Once your heart ignites with passion, you will be able to pass the torch to others. People need to hear your message, for as Dame Edith Sitwell (1887-1964) wrote, "The poet speaks to all men of that other life of theirs that they have smothered and forgotten." Similarly, Johann Wolfgang von Goethe (1749-1832) said, "A man should hear a little music, read a little poetry, and see a fine picture every day of his life, in order that worldly cares may not obliterate the sense of the beautiful which God has implanted in the human soul."
8. Is something disturbing you? Are you going through a painful experience? What better way to get it out of your system than by writing poetry? Poetry is cathartic. It allows you to transfer the pain from your mind to a sheet of paper. And as you focus on the rhyme, rhythm, and resonance of the poem you are creating, all thoughts of pain recede, much like the ebb tide. Pain has given birth to some of the finest works of art and is a perfect example of how we can extract something positive from even the most negative circumstances.

Does becoming a poet, such as the one I describe, appear to be beyond your reach? Well, the ability to write poetry is innate. That is, it is as natural as walking. True, those who spend time practicing can walk more gracefully, but most of us can walk with little or no effort. The same is true for poetry. We can write it if we try. However, a little guidance will make our efforts much more fruitful. Here are some books that can help:

1. *The Art & Craft of Poetry* by Michael J. Bugeja, Writer's Digest Books, 1994.
2. *How to Write Poetry* by Nancy Bogen, 1998.
3. *Complete Idiot's Guide to Writing Poetry* by Nikki Moustaki, 2001.
4. *The Practice of Poetry: Writing Exercises From Poets Who Teach* by Robin Behn, 1992.
5. *In the Palm of Your Hand: The Poet's Portable Workshop* by Steve Kowit, 1995.

29

Learn from Everything that Comes Your Way

She was a very quiet, modest, middle-aged lady. He was a young clergyman, probably in his early thirties, who was sitting beside her in the midtown doctor's office. I was there in the same room, reading my book, hoping to kill time while waiting to see my practitioner.

I'll admit my crime: I couldn't concentrate on the book. I was listening to the conversation between these two people. I know, my behavior was totally unacceptable, but I hope that the quiet lady and young priest will forgive me. I hope!

"Why me again, Father? Why is this happening to me? Is there any answer to my question? Tell me, please, what have I done so badly in my life to `deserve' such poor health?"

A thousand-year-old question: "Why do bad things happen to good people?"

Who knows the answer?

The words were an expression of emotional pain and a cry of anguish. I knew any rational explanation would be irrelevant; he knew an expression of pain required empathy.

What was he going to say?

"All events serve precisely for what we need at that time. Sometimes in life adversity can be a wake-up call, encouraging us to learn, not to punish us. If you have an acceptance and understanding that a human life consists of moments of happiness and moments of sadness, during the time of sadness you will know that there is another side of it. Everything that happens to us happens for a reason. There is a purpose and meaning to the difficult times we face. It's part of our soul's journey. Some experiences may seem bad at that moment, only because we lack the perspective of the bigger picture."

I couldn't stop thinking about that conversation. No, it wasn't a conversation; it was a sermon in the midtown doctor's office.

"What's this? Is he teaching her the lesson or is he comforting her?"

It was not up to me to make any judgmental thoughts. I was there as an "intruder".

The lady didn't say anything.

I heard his soft voice saying: "Events in our life are not mere coincidences, nothing just happens; there is always a powerful lesson to learn. Still, life's fullness isn't stripped away just because you're going through a difficult time. When something bad happens, the first step should be to try to understand the message, not to suffer. It's our obligation and wisdom to figure out the message, and move forward. It's hard to understand and accept, but it's true."

"I know and understand that, Father, but help me to heal this emptiness within me. I have no confidence in my abilities."

"You have a power within you. I know that. The emotional healing will take place only when you learn to accept and experience the full range of your feelings. The true healing lies in self-acceptance. I believe that every one of us is born into life with the inner power and possibility to experience prosperity.

Every individual has a unique mission to fulfill. Our soul has a purpose in this life. No matter what happens, look for the good. When you seek it, you will find it."

I posed a question to myself: "Where am I, in a church or in the midtown office? What's wrong with this place today?"

The priest didn't raise his voice when he said:

"Early in my seminary, I accepted that life is always trying to teach us exactly what we need to learn. Whatever happened to me, I saw it as a gift and a lesson to learn. The more I've learned and the more I've accepted, the more freedom, wholeness and satisfaction I've experienced. When a bad thing happened to me, ten years ago, I could either check out from life or move forward and grow. I chose God as my choice. Everyone has their own challenges, and I learned from my own."

I heard the announcement: "Father, please, the doctor is waiting for you."

"Just one more thing, before I go," said the young priest in a wheelchair, "I can't remember who, but someone wisely said:

`When life becomes a battleground, your mind is your best weapon.'"

The lesson was over. The young ill priest and the middle-aged lady would probably never meet again. Everyone needs to learn the lesson for themselves.

I still was there, in shock!

What a powerful lesson I learned today in that midtown room, listening to this conversation. We need to know how to accept defeat when it is not possible to win, and also, we need to fight under any given conditions!

How to choose our strategy?

Whatever the outcome of our strategy is, be thankful and grateful for what you have done. Give yourself credit for facing challenges in life and connect to your spiritual essence.

We are limited only by our own thoughts and beliefs.

30

Are you on the Right Track?

It's never too late to understand what's going on in your life.

Are you on the right track? You don't know? I'll help you if you feel you are working harder and harder, but gaining less and less out of life. You definitely need to read this article, just as a starting point.

I've spent a lot of time trying to understand what's the most important thing to do to get a satisfied life. I have done my homework and this article is just a small part of the information I have. I hope you will find it useful. By the end of reading it, I do hope your mind will be clearer. You will be learning more about turning points and what influences your life.

My subject is very simple; how to lead a meaningful life and what leads us to live a life out of balance. By being aware of these factors, people can escape running their own life with no direction. Are you ready to sit down and spend time and energy planning for your future? If you do, planning for the future will take time, but it will be worth it.

Do you have your own system of personal goals, with a clear direction where your life is heading, including what steps you need to take? If not, I am afraid you are wasting your time exposing yourself to painful discoveries. Late in your life, the only answer could be: I am sorry, but it is too late for you.

If there is one thing you want to get in life, it's your concept. I know for sure that every successful person in any given field is successful because he had a concept, knowing where he was heading. Without it, you won't be able to find your way and how to express your true self. Your personal concept will decide how far you can go in your life and how successful will you be.

Maybe you don't believe that having a concept and a clear picture of what you want out of your life will give you any advantage. If you still have a question why it is so important to have a direction and a concept where you would like to be in life I'll give you one reason. The reason is very easy to understand and accept. When you know direction, your intellectual centre will provide you with information, ideas, suggestions and the right thoughts to reach your destination. Yes, whatever you do, your mind will be there for you to satisfy yourself and give you support. You just need to understand your true abilities. When you know yourself and when you have a concept in life, you are on the right track.

If you don't know your direction, or if you don't have direction, then find a purpose in life. For a "solid" life you need a solid point. Having purpose is a solid point. It will give you a sense of direction and meaning whatever you want to be. Remember, we are always responsible for the path we are taking. Don't be discouraged if the outcome you get is not always positive.

The other day I saw a person who went to see a professional counsellor "for a concept and direction". Wrong! The only person who can make your goal, concept or direction is you. If you are following someone else's direction, with the best intentions, you are on the wrong track.

Of course, we need suggestions from our parents, families, friends, colleagues and professionals. But, they are there just to help us lay out our own concept. Choose your concept very carefully; you don't want to live someone else's life.

Your current position in life is inevitably a byproduct of your previous homework. I know, you got a raw material from your parents, environment, society and other circumstances in your life, but no one would want to live life with raw materials. You must make your own life out of raw materials. It doesn't matter what your educational background is, your type of character or your IQ; all you need is in your hands. As you know "If you get a lemon in a life, make lemonade of it". This is very true and we need to respect it.

Successful, happy people followed their concept, not only their nose, or maybe you still believe they only follow their nose with their life, job and other people? What are you following? You have a choice. It's up to you.

Consequently, today's business world is full of people involved in careers that were consuming but not fulfilling. If you want to avoid that kind of career situation you need to know the answers to these simple questions: Who are you? What are you good at? What's your concept? What's your direction in life? If you know the answers, you are on the right track and more importantly you will be relieved from stress.

How do you to make a good concept and what do you include in your concept?

Try to include in it some general premises. For instance, ask yourself; what are my personal abilities? Where's my main field of interest? What's my goal in life? What's my personality type?

Learn your strongest skills and values.

Making a concept is a long term task. Try to make long term decisions, not short ones. Short term decisions will give you only a temporarly "feel good" opinion about yourself.

Obviously, everyone wants the best life in all circumstances, but how many of us take care of our concept and direction? No plan, no goals, no concept - no satisfied life. Why don't you want to plan your life? If on our way through life we feel that something is missing out there, don't blame life. We need to do what we have to do, one way or another.

I know everyone wants to live a successful life. What is a successful life?

Simply, when you focus on what's inside you, not only what's outside, you live a successful life. By a successful life I mean a responsible, meaningful, thankful, creative, spiritual life. Not an empty life full of jealousy, competition, anger and stress.

Make your life full of health not just wealth, understand what's important to you, not to anyone else. At any given moment you need to know what you have done with your life, and what you should be doing now. Creating a healthy, successful, hopeful, and joyful life out of any given circumstances will allow you to gain responsibility for yourself and your family.

Good luck!

31

Change is Good

We fear change. Any change, whether it is good or bad, is always anxiety producing. All changes cause some discomfort. Of course, we do not like anxiety and we do not want to change anything.

Therefore, we need the courage to change our bad habits and negative behavior. We use our anxiety as an excuse for not changing. We are always trying to do the same things, expecting to get something different. Unfortunately, that is impossible. We have to pay a price for changing ourselves. But, it is worth it.

The only thing we have to do is to give up some of our ways of thinking and acting. We have to stop avoiding changing.

Yes, it can be very difficult, but we have to try, anyway. Our own resistance behavior keeps us from moving ahead. Moving ahead means changing. The opposite means being stuck. Being stuck is bad and creates a sad feeling. If you want to grow - change yourself. The only way to break this cycle is to make changes.

One way to change another person is to change yourself first.

When changing yourself, you will change others who surround you.

Some people would rather remain with their limitations than give up what they are getting from being anxious.

Get out of your comfort zone and make it happen. Think of your process of changing as exciting. Open a new door in the wall of limitations. Fear of failure? That is normal. Deal with your problems, bad habits, fears, and limitations. Direct your life.

Start with small things.

Our resistance to change is our excuse not to grow up. We do not want to take responsibility for our own happiness or lack of it!

Hard to believe, but it's true.

Do not maintain your negative behavior! If you want to change your bad behavior, start changing yourself today. Not tomorrow, but today.

Procrastination is another excuse for not changing. When we do not want to do something - we procrastinate. Do what you have to do today. Be responsible and change your bad habits. Very soon you will find yourself in a totally different world - the world of happiness.

Before starting to make any changes we have to let go of our negative and skeptical attitude, for it is self-defeating. If we say, "No, it will not work," do not be surprised if it doesn't.

We will have a hard time letting go of this condition. Be open- minded and recognize your resistance pattern.

Often, people make the mistake of over-analyzing and intellectualizing. If you really want to change yourself, do not be so analytical. Analytical behavior produces more anxiety, depression and confusion. Understand it is just our subconscious that wants to resist.

Accept changes as a process and do not feel sorry for yourself.

Learn to like and to respect yourself, not to feel sorry for yourself. You are not different and your problem is not the worst.

I know what you are saying now, "Can we change everything in the world for the better?" Of course not. But if you cannot change something - accept it.

Be secure in yourself. Insecure behavior is another problem for people who do not want to change bad habits. They will always find a reason for not changing. For instance, they may say:

"People may not like me with all my changes, so I will stay the same."

Again, this is just another excuse! And you know what, if you do not like to change anything, you will feel worse - not better!

Continuing in the same bad behavior will kill you. I am telling you the truth.

You can end up in severe depression with a lot of anxiety and fears, and you can get physically ill from anxiety and depression.

We choose our behavior. Everything is up to us! Choose to start changing your habits today! I am not saying that is an easy process. Not at all. You might feel lost and confused. That is okay. Get over this condition.

You don't need your anxiety, fears, depression or bad mood.

You have a choice: would you prefer to stay suffering with anxiety and depression or prefer to accept the anxiety of changing?

What is your choice? Which way makes you feel better? Which is worst? Neither is pleasant! It is up to you.

Please, try to change yourself and try to accept yourself. Gain self-control and peace of mind will be yours. Trust me!

32

Do You Like Yourself?

If you believe everyone loves himself, you are wrong. I know this sounds strange, but many people really do not like themselves, or you might even say they hate themselves.

Unfortunately, they are missing a very important ingredient of life. Our experience provides us with thousands of examples.

Not feeling love for oneself will produce problems.

Do not treat yourself badly!

For good mental and physical health, we need to love ourselves.

If you have love for yourself, you have love for others as well.

Only when you experience love for yourself can you truly love others. You cannot offer something to others that you do not have. Everything begins with love. Love is an art and the key to happiness and success. Love is the ingredient that binds everything together. Fortunately, we can learn to love ourselves.

Learning to love ourselves will make us more compassionate and we will enjoy life more.

I am not saying become preoccupied with yourself. Just treat yourself with respect, especially in failure. Learn to accept your limits. We are human beings and we make mistakes at times.

After all, no matter how impressed you are with others the fact is: You are much more important than any VIP. So why not treat yourself at least as well as you would treat them? When you love yourself, you do things for yourself in a more natural way. The greater your love, the more positive it is. Love always makes itself available to those who ask.

If you want to change something in your life, you need to love yourself. If love is lacking, the change will be limited. Without knowing yourself and loving yourself you cannot use the power of love. People learn how incredible they are by learning to love themselves.

We, as imperfect human beings, need our own loving support. When you love who you are, you automatically bring out the best in you. Love yourself enough to allow yourself to feel your emotions. Always take care of yourself.

Why is it so important to love yourself? The answer is very simple. If you love yourself, you will not reject yourself and no one else will either, or if they do, it certainly will not matter to you.

If you believe you have so called "faults" inside you, it will be difficult to love yourself. Building love for yourself builds your self-worth. Life is about change. Events come and go, but the love that you have for yourself is constant, and it is the most important asset you possess in your life. When you love yourself you are more lovable.

Why I am writing about this topic? Because the most important factor determining the richness of our life is in the way we perceive ourselves. And if you do not like yourself, please remember you are who you are; you are doing the best you can.

Just love who you are and accept yourself.

Often the best contribution you can make in life is to work on yourself. Love is always a life force and energy. Your opinion of yourself is more important than what others think of you. You need to like yourself if you want to treat yourself better. You do not have to be a great achiever in life to feel love for yourself. Happy people like themselves! Where love is, there is healing and energy.

33

How to Get along with people

Have you ever thought about this very simple question: how do you get along with people? Are you successful in getting along with others or are you struggling with everyone in your life? Do you have the ability to be a good listener? Have you ever read a book or article on the subject of getting along with people - an art and skill we ought to learn about?

We all need to learn and understand the very effective skill involved in getting along with people. If you are not very familiar with it, don't shift the responsibility for conducting a conversation to others and don't blame events for your less than optimum ability.

Maybe it's time to learn more about human knowledge regarding how to understand and deal with people. Maybe one day your life might be totally different just because you improved your approach to other people.

In this article I am going to explore how we can improve our ability to deal even with "difficult" people.

First, start your conversation with a thorough preparation of your thoughts. Put a smile on your face and stay positive. A smile is so powerful I can't stress its significance enough. It is a messenger of your goodwill and costs nothing. The expression on your face is more important than anything else.

Even when talking on the phone you need to smile; your smile comes through your voice! This is a simple way of saying you are a friendly person who is ready to accept the presence and communication of the other person.

Getting along with people and knowing how to influence is knowledge. These days we talk about the time it takes to gain knowledge; there is much technical stuff we have to learn each day, but even more important is our education in the art of influencing people. If you want to improve your skills and knowledge of how to get along with people around you, it is necessary to understand human nature.

If you want to get along with others and be a good conversationalist, learn first to be a good listener and give the other person a chance to say what he/she wants to say. Naturally, the tendency is to talk mostly about ourselves, about subjects that interest us, always from our point of view on any given topic.

If you are ready to listen to the person who is talking to you with exclusive attention, you are on your way to creating a good friendship with almost anyone. Respect and encourage others to talk about themselves and accept them as they are, rather than as you wish them to be. Acceptance of others will bring you tranquility and an inner peace instead of anger and resentment.

You cannot force everyone to be polite, but you can do your best.

People always think of themselves and like themselves much more than they like anyone in the world. Therefore, talk to people about them and they will listen to you for hours, complimenting you on your conversation even if you didn't say a word! Just listening to the other person, you will give them a feeling of importance.

Never forget, people are struggling for a feeling of importance. Become interested in other people's lives; do not try to get other people interested in you. In conversation, frequently use the pronoun "you," rather than "I." Use frequently the personal pronoun "you", not "I". When dealing with people, we should always remember we are dealing with creatures of emotions and prejudices rather than with creatures of logic.

Speaking of human nature, our understanding is greater when we deal with what we want as opposed to what others want. Every act we have performed was performed because we wanted to do it. Sounds very egotistical-but it's true. So the only way to influence others is to talk about what they want. Next time when you go for a job interview, remember to ask yourself what the company wants from you, not what you want from the company. Use that skill for everything and you will be the beneficiary of everything in the world.

Yes, you have to be interested in people—the company, or whatever—if you want to be successful in getting what you want. I am not writing fiction; this is reality. We are in charge of our relationships with people and we are responsible for our ability to accept others.

If you are really interested in talking to others and interested in making good friendships, do not begin any conversation with subjects on which you differ. Start with things on which you agree. If in the first 5 minutes of conversation you say "no" more than twice, I can predict with good confidence that your conversation will end up in Nowhere City.

The difference between a good conversation and a bad one depends on two words: "yes "and "no," both having a huge impact on the future of your relationship with that person. " No" is much more potent than you think. The "no" response is a more difficult handicap to surmount than you might imagine.

Saying "no "to the other person means, "you are not right," "you don't know," "you don't understand," "you are not knowledgeable," and sometimes even, "I don't like you!"

"No" creates a reaction in one's entire body, throughout the nervous, muscular, and glandular systems. The body is under stress, ready for fight. And next time when you see the same person, your body will remember these physiological reactions. On the other hand, with "yes," none of the above activities take place.

If your question is how it's possible always to agree with someone, which is an impossible task, remember to express your criticism as advice, always respecting a person's right to see the situation in another way. Never tell anyone they are wrong.

They will want to strike back, they will not change their minds, and in the end you will have an enemy instead of a friend. If you want to prove something, do it in such a manner so that no one thinks you are doing it. If you start your disagreement with the feeling you need to teach someone, or with the intention of proving you are right, it doesn't work—simply because you cannot teach anyone anything. The only thing you can do is help them find the truth within themselves. Do not be aggressive or act superior.

I am not trying to say leave people with their (to your thinking) false opinions and wrong statements, not at all. What I am trying to say is speak politely, saying something like: "from my understanding," or "maybe you are right and I am wrong, but I think." or just simply "I see this situation," or "I am not an expert in that particular field, but ...."

For me, the most important thing is: if you are wrong, admit it; do not pretend to know everything. You are, just as everyone else, a human being who makes mistakes. There are thousands of ways to leave the other person with dignity and let him/her feel worthy and clever but, before you try to teach or correct someone, try to understand him/her and make a decision to understand, instead of correcting. I know it is much easier to criticize than understand the other person's point of view. In one word, criticism is useless, it's a very dangerous weapon, and criticizing will not correct the situation we condemn.

What should we do? I do not have a prescription for every situation; simply try different approaches; for example, try to explain in a pleasant tone of voice, why it is beneficial for them, not for you, to do a certain thing in the manner you suggest. The only way of changing something in the other person is by inspiring enthusiasm and a desire in them to change, while maintaining the feeling of respect for their own beliefs.

Whenever you are in dilemma regarding how to react, ask yourself how you would feel or react if you were in the other person's shoes. Your degree of successful conversation is proportional to the amount of control you have over your thoughts and feelings.

34

I am Grateful for

I know, I can hear you saying, "I am not thankful for anything in my life. I have no a reason to be thankful for... and so on."

I know, you feel down with no energy for the day. You feel sorry for yourself, with no desire to change anything in your life!

But I know you are wrong, and I will try telling you why you are.

First, your statement is expressed in extremes. The situation is never totally "bad." It is not always easy to see something useful in a "bad situation." I know that, but it can be very valuable to understand the benefits of any situation. If you can do that, you will improve your mental health. For sure!

Second, your unpleasant feelings have nothing to do with reality.

Your view of yourself is an opinion, not a fact, and opinions can be biased and mistaken. The good news is that opinions can be changed!

You feel terrible and you see everything from a distorted point of view. Currently, you are a different person.

A combination of thoughts that are in conflict with reality produces destructive mental energy. This mental energy generates very unpleasant sensations in your body. We call them emotions, like fear, anxiety, anger and guilt. All these emotions have negative impacts on your body.

The very first answer to your feelings about yourself is to change your way of thinking to a more positive approach. By changing your mental attitude, you will change the condition of your life. Every act in your life is the direct outcome of a certain fixed belief. For that reason you need a positive viewpoint. Therefore, remember that you cannot escape the result of your thoughts.

With "negative frequencies" you will attract others who are resonating at similar levels. Yes, we create our surroundings.

Feel positive if you want to be surrounded with positive people.

Further, if you want to feel happy, and I know you do, act as a happy person. Just pretending to be happy can change the situation for the better. This is a proven fact, not wishful thinking. Happy thoughts will cause your intellectual centre to send happy messages to your awareness, and thankful thoughts are those happy messages!

Can you change yourself for the better with more thankful thoughts? Your strategy and coping technique will change dramatically if you can do a very easy exercise when you are feeling down!

Can you do it for the sake of your children, spouse, your relatives or your friends? For the sake of the people who love you, and for the sake of your own health? Can you? If you can, you will help...yourself.

What I am asking you to do is a small task, an exercise that has been known for many years.

The exercise is:

Whenever you feel down or worry too much, sit down in a quiet place, take a pen and piece of paper and start writing. Write for at least 15 minutes all the things that you are thankful for.

Write down whatever comes to your mind. Be very specific with all the details, names, and times. Do not think the list is too long!

Do not pay attention to the grammar or style. Just express your thankfulness. When you finish writing, read over the things you just wrote. Read aloud! Finally, say, "Thank you. I am grateful."

This small exercise can change your life. It works!

Now, I am going to explain why this exercise works.

Whenever you are writing something on paper about yourself, you are sending messages to your subconscious. Your subconscious will accept whatever you are saying to yourself, without checking or arguing with you!

By giving uplifting, positive thoughts to your subconscious, you will produce so called "positive energy." With positive energy in your mind you will be able to think differently, more positively.

By changing your attitude, you will find many other ways to solve your problems and overcome obstacles. Your mind will become clear and be ready to give you new ideas on what to do. You will gain new motivation and meaning.

Armed with new motivation, you will be able to do whatever you want to.

You need to do this small exercise to get out of the blues and stop the worrisome "what if" thinking.

The only person in the world who can do it for you is you. You are the best therapist for yourself! Nobody knows you better than you do. But, you need to do this small exercise.

35

"I Hope You Dance"

Have you heard the above titled beautiful song by Leann Rimes, lyrics by Mark D Sanders and Tia Sillers?

"Whenever one door closes, I hope one more opens. Promise me that you will give faith a fighting chance. And when you get the choice to sit it out or dance, I hope you dance."

I really hope you will dance and not sit it out. I hope you will. Live each day and each year of your life to the fullest so that you will have hope and look forward with confidence and back with no regrets.

With hope and optimism everything depends on you. Do not be afraid to be happy. Having hope gives you the strength to understand that absolute certainty never arrives.

Your best companion in life is your own hope. Keep your hope with you at all times. The ability to live with hope through everything in life is a great inspiration and provides strength and knowledge.

Hope is the most important healing force. Hope of recovery, hope of loving and being loved. Never say there is no hope. When there is no hope, there is no life. Better to say, "Where there is no hope, I will build it." With hope, your mental attitude and your personality will develop a better life and destiny.

With great hope you will face the future optimistically.

It's terribly important that we hang on to hope and never call a brownout a burnout. When there is a temporary overload on the emotional system, do not lose hope. Just rest, a new dawn will arrive.

I am talking about attitudes such as Hope, Optimism, and a Positive outlook. Perhaps we do not yet understand the human mind and body enough to provide answers why hope and optimism are so beneficial to us.

But they are!

What is HOPE?

Hope is the belief that you will be able to meet your goals and the expectation of good things. The desire for something good is the basis for believing that good will come. With Hope one believes that all obstacles are challenges rather than dead ends.

Focusing on personal hope will help us develop a more positive, goal-oriented thinking.

If you can believe it, you can achieve it.

The best medicine in the world is hope, a positive attitude, and optimism.

In these days we really need more medical doctors who will prescribe hope and optimism as medicine. Optimists are healthy people because our health depends on our hope. Hope is a force with a powerful influence.

Discouragement, negativism, and hopelessness will sap you of the power to act.

And people who don't act are like dead people.

We need to learn how to fight pessimism and bring more optimism and hope into our life.

We all suffer various trials in life, some of us more than others. Why do some people try and try again, whereas others seem to give up after relatively minor difficulties?

The way of thinking can make the difference.

If you have thoughts such as, "I am a total failure" or "I am of no use to anybody" you are putting a big "STOP" sign in front of you. No actions, no solutions, and no power lead to a lot of excuses.

Fight back your pessimism. Say to yourself, "I know my negative thoughts are destructive. I am going to fight them."

You are right, because your pessimistic thoughts are your overreactions. You are catastrophizing. Push aside negative thinking.

When you lose a job or money or an opportunity, you are losing a lot. But when you lose hope, you are losing everything.

With hope you can gain anything. Do not lose hope.

Hopelessness is a sickness that goes together with pessimism, depression, apathy, and anxiety.

Today many medical doctors believe in the value of hope as therapy. " Hope is a powerful therapy," asserts Dr. W. Gifford.

They know, for patients with hope and support survive longer and suffer less pain.

Consider a study on the role of optimism and pessimism in coronary heart disease.

A researcher comments, "Most of the evidence shows thinking positively is good for your health". This study provides some of the first hard medical evidence for this idea in the arena of cardiology.

Hope and optimism are crucial not just for health. Even longevity has been linked to optimism. When older people were exposed to fleeting messages linking the aging process with increased wisdom and experience, they were later found to walk with increased strength and energy.

36

What's Your Personality?

What's more important for your personal success; your educational background and job skills or your personality? If your answer is education, of course, then I need to disappoint you!

Our personality determines our life experience, shapes our performance and consequently, determines our success or failure.

Job success or failure, and job satisfaction, depend on our personality. Even our relationship with our spouse, colleagues and ourselves depends on our personal traits.

We are good at something only when we are operating from our strengths. We can achieve excellence and manage ourselves only by using our strong personal traits, not our weaknesses.

We are here in our current situation because of our personality type and traits, not for any other reason. We can simply say that everything depends on personality.

How important is it to know your personality? Knowing your personality has many benefits, because personality colors everything in a person's life. If you want to understand your direction and what's happening in your life, you need to know your personality first. If you want success in any area of life, you need to know your personality inventory first. Self-evaluation will help gain a better understanding of how to behave, think, react, and respond to any life situation. When you recognize patterns in yourself, then you can take control of yourself by choosing to react differently, more positively, I hope. We need to learn how to control our emotions, feelings, and habits, and how to deal with life itself and with other people.

Only if you know yourself well can you change for the better any of your given traits.

I have learned a lot about character and personality from a young fellow who has applied for a new job. No need to wonder: I'll explain everything in detail.

This young fellow is a very well educated person with little work experience. He wanted to change his career by switching to a new very demanding field. To reach his goal he has applied for a new position and has gotten an interview.

I met him just a couple days after his second interview.

Fortunately, he got the new job. He was thrilled, not just because of getting a better job, but because he now knows his strengths and knows where he belongs! What was the reason for such excitement? The answer is very simple, he has "discovered" himself after taking a Personality Inventories Test. He now knows himself much better than before, and knows what he should correct.

This article explains what I've learned, in general, on personality.

First, I need to clarify the word "personality". In this article I am not talking about personality as "a person of considerable prominence," such as a Hollywood personality. My intention is to explore personality as a description of personal attributes or a set of characteristics temperamental, mental, emotional, and behavioral. Personality, which means "mask" in Greek, is actually a person's natural mask.

In this article I am not talking about personality disorder, which generally are life long disturbances, I am just giving general thoughts on personality.

Our personality originates during childhood, and is shaped by our family and life circumstances and, of course, by our biological make up. Personality is a set of beliefs about the world and is an integral part of the person.

Just to show how important a factor personality is in everyone's life, I'll give you this statement "Studies show that personality can propel a person of fairly average intelligence and education to great heights, or can make the smartest person feel like a failure."

Being master of your life simply means being master of your personality. Interestingly, people usually do not pay attention to mastering their personality. More often they try to master education and job skills, but not personality. Each and any task in life requires the right personality, talent and skills. It's our responsibility to find out our traits and where our personality, talent and skills fit. How a person performs, and what he is good at or not, is a matter of nature, not just knowledge and/or skills.

Yes, I know we can slightly change our performance in some area, but it's definitely not easy to completely change our personality.

If you take a personality self-profile or self-assessment test, the results will give you a snapshot of your personality. For instance, you will learn how sociable and helpful you are. Are you a dependent, tense, rigid, or maybe, controlling person?

Maybe you are always looking for approval? How competitive, innovative, achieving or conscientious are you? How is your anger profile? Do you have very little difficulty maintaining your focus on a task? I hope you are not a perfectionist, or a depressed or anxious person.

An assertiveness test will help you answer the question "Are you a human doormat?" Do you say "yes" when you mean "no"? What about your stress tolerance level? You probably are good at coping skills, but don't know it! I do hope your self esteem and self confidence are okay.

If you have a high score in the worry or obsessive compulsive category, you need to do something about it very soon! Is your attitude and expectation category low or high? I know you have no problem with the emotions category, but what about your social situations category?

Learn everything you can about your own personality and try to correct your weaknesses. Remember always to place yourself where you can make a great contribution and produce good results. Take care of your bad habits. Knowing your bad habits can help you improve your performance and reach achievements. If you know your test results for all your traits, then you are on your way to mastering your life.

Learn first who you are!

37

Media Related Stress

The media plays a big role in our stressful life, making us stressful, every single day.

Why is that? There are many explanations, but my concern is that we live in a really stressful western world and do not need media related stress. We want to reduce our stress, not to increase it.

For many of the media, the only good news is bad news. Have you ever seen on TV any "good breaking news "? If it is good news, it is not "breaking news".

When you feel fearful and anxious watching all these catastrophes, you will want to learn more of the details. This is all about control! The media needs our attention, making us desperately stressed-out and depressed. The media bosses are always looking for "a critical mass of catastrophes "to keep us occupied.

Have a look at the lead story headlines. What you see or hear is only disasters, only bad news and frustrations.

Why are at least 60% of all headlines about catastrophes? The answer is very simple, people like to read about tragedies! I am surprised! I have asked myself, why do people want to see or hear about bad news? Why do they want to know about someone they don't know? Do they believe they are helping the people who are in trouble?

I don't know the answer to all these questions and I am not blaming people. They are used to doing that! People's desire to learn about disasters is part of human nature. I was surprised when I have learned, that human beings use their biological systems to save themselves! Experts say: When you pay attention to other people's adversity, you will keep the same thing from happening to you! Our interest in disasters is a matter of self-preservation.

Very interesting! My question is: Why does the media misuse the power of our natural biological system? The problem with watching bad news is that when we look at people suffering, our bodies react in the same way. When we see a person in pain, it will activate the pain-sensitive regions of our own brain. Human brains are equipped with "mirror neurons" to help us mimic the people around us. It's part of our genetic heritage. The media understands the meaning of control, and how to use it to control us.

In our body we have the so called "control buttons." These "buttons" will help us our stress under control. But, if we have no control, or if we have little control, the stress will get to us. By watching all these adversities we have no control at all.

Because we have no control, we experience fear, stress and anxiety!

That is the reality of human nature.

The media understands human physiology. Their motto is: "If you like to see disasters, we will provide you with disasters."

The media doesn't care about people's stress. They care only about profit. Profit from us, imperfect human beings.

Instead of spending your time watching disasters, spend your time searching for more productive, positive stories.

We need to teach people that life is about happiness, too, not just about disasters. We need to teach people how to make life more joyful, more useful, not more stressful.

I am not an utopist or an idealist. I realize life is unpredictable, imperfect, and full of uncertainty. Life is not always fair, and has no obligation to be fair. But, we don't need the media to remind us, constantly, day in and day out.

Now, I have a question for you: What kind of life do you expect from people who watch only "bad news," nothing but images of people suffering? Do you expect them to be positive, happy and satisfied?

What you can expect is people with stress, anxiety, and confused emotions!

My point is: Please, stop watching stressful and fearful news!

Get a life! You don't need to know all the "bad news" from all over the world. You have enough "news" to deal with in your own life. You will not improve the quality of your life watching late-night news. If you want to reduce stress in your life, try to avoid all the sensationalized stories of violence in the media.

Learn to ignore what you cannot control.

Instead of watching bad news try to learn more about things you can control. Give yourself a sense of control and you will be less stressful, happier, more satisfied, and more productive.

I wish you a life with no media related stress.

38

Mind Power

"The Eagle who thought he was a chicken"

"A man found an eagle's egg and put it in a nest of a barnyard hen. The eaglet hatched with the brood of chicks and grew up with them. All his life the eagle did what the barnyard chicks did, thinking he was a barnyard chicken.

"Years passed and the eagle grew old. One day he saw a magnificent bird above him in the cloudless sky. The old eagle looked up in awe. 'Who's that?' he asked.

"'That's the eagle, the king of the birds,' said his neighbor. 'He belongs to the sky. We belong to the earth; we're chickens.'

"So the eagle lived and died as chicken, for that's what he thought he was." (By Anthony de Mello, S.J.)

I don't remember ever reading a more powerful and brilliant fable. Actually this isn't a fable, but a textbook about the power of mind and thoughts. It is about fate, destiny, low self-esteem, low self-confidence, and comfort zones. In short, this is a story about human life.

We are our thoughts. Mind is power! It is always there, but it's not always used. Yes, we often don't take advantage of the power within us. What a pity! Why don't we fully use the power of our mind? Because we don't believe in it! We need to learn to believe in the power of mind or it will not be able to help us.

Everyone has heard that the mind can do many things and that it is powerful. In fact it is so powerful that it can also be dangerous. For example, doctors and therapists know that effective treatments will not work for patients that do not believe in the treatments.

Mind power is spiritual power. It can help! But it only helps those who help themselves. There is a connection between the body and mind, a strong and powerful connection. If we decide to live healthy, happy, and successful lives, the mind is there to help us do so.

The mind and body are one. The most important fact is that our mind controls our body. You probably are familiar with the computer expression "Garbage in, Garbage out." That is, what we put into the computer is what we get out of it. The results are based on what we feed into it. The same is true for us.

Feed your mind with positive thoughts. If we feed our mind with thoughts of love, peace and joy, we will enjoy happy lives. Positive thoughts help and protect us. They are programs that resist disease. But thoughts of hate, anxiety, anger, fear, and despair are programs that produce disease.

Do you know which emotion is the most positive? LOVE. Any kind of love is helpful, not just personal or family love. Love is a powerful emotion! You want to feel happy? Then smile! Smile in every situation. Find a reason to smile. Act as a happy, positive person, despite all the negative circumstances in your life. Acting as a positive person will produce happy thoughts. Our mind-body connection will send these happy thoughts to our awareness. And this will create feelings of happiness.

Do you accept that your feelings depend on how you think? The field of CBT (cognitive behavioral therapy) is based on this principle. There is an old saying that "Nothing is good or bad, but thinking makes it so." Everything positive or negative, good or bad, that we say to ourselves are suggestions that program our mind.

Choose to focus on the positive! Look for the good; expect good and you will get good. Today we know an important fact: Our brain cannot tell the difference between a real or imagined experience!!! That's why visualization, affirmations and meditation work!

When we use our imagination, our brain will accept the images in our mind as real. Our thoughts create our reality. So, if we can manage our thoughts, we will be able to create and control our future. Self-talk is a valuable tool. Talk to your mind. You may not believe in it, but it works. We become what we think about.

Do you want to be successful? Of course you do! Then watch your thoughts. They determine your attitude, which determine your motivation, which, in turn, determine your performance. Our performance depends on our way of thinking. Whether we succeed or not is based on our thoughts and beliefs. The ability to think big and positive is a key to a successful and happy life. Positive thinking guides our performance, success and intelligence. We are products of our own thoughts.

Our memory bank stores each and every thought. Refuse to deposit anything in it other than positive thoughts. Repeat your positive thoughts over and over again. If you think you cannot change your thoughts, you are wrong! You can, but it requires an effort. Is it easy? Not at all. It will take months, or even years to change your attitude by changing your way of thinking. However, there is only one way of thinking that is OK. And that is the positive way!

It is easy to prove that you can change your emotions by managing them. Just act the way you want to feel. Start with a big, sincere smile. A big smile can beat anxiety, fear, and despair.

Start your day with positive uplifting affirmations! Say to yourself every day that you feel wonderful and happy, and you will begin to feel that way.

Use words as tools. If you choose the right words you will produce positive mental images. Look at things not as they are now, but as they can be tomorrow. Visualize your happiness. Believing in something sets the mind in motion to find a way to bring it about. The role of our mind is to help us. Its function is to manifest our beliefs.

Do you want to control your feelings and stress? Then, CONTROL YOUR THOUGHTS. Our feelings come from our thoughts. Stress is a feeling. Yes, by controlling our thoughts, we can control stress. Stress comes from our thinking.

Low self-esteem and low self-confidence will determine how others react to you. People will see in you what you see in yourself. Self-talk is a mirror for the world around you. You are what you think you are. A positive attitude can make things better. But a negative attitude will always make things worse.

It is important for good health to we use the minds to think positively. Your outlook affects your body's chemistry. The best medicine in the world is positive thinking. Don't be "The Eagle who thought he was a chicken."

39

Perfectionist's Personality

Who Wants To Be A Perfectionist?

Being loser! I know nobody wants to be a loser but for a perfectionist his consciousness tells him: you are a loser if you cannot be perfect, successful, and the number one achiever. What he achieves is more important than who he is. For him life has no value unless he is Number One. Simply, the perfectionist has learned early in life that other people valued him because of how much he achieved. As a result, he has learned to value himself only because of other's approval.

Fear of failure, disapproval or making mistakes are perfectionist's nightmares!

They don't want to accept a simple statement: I am a human being prone to error, frailty, and imperfections. No, perfectionist is driven by an intense need to avoid failure and mistakes. This is a set of self-defeating thoughts and behaviors.

Idealism, driven by an intense need to avoid failure is always in a perfectionist's mind. He must always reach the ideal in everything, because it is the ideal that gives his life a meaning. If he is not able to accomplish things in a perfect or ideal way, he won't start at all and he will give up his goal.

This is his way of trying to protect himself from criticism, rejection, and disapproval.

A deep feeling of inferiority is another characteristic of a perfectionist. Lack of belief in himself and knowing that he will never be able to achieve an idyllic goal can lead a perfectionist to lose the belief in self. He is not able to live with himselves.

Pessimism and depression are the consequences of perfectionism.

Needless is to say that always being perfect is an impossible task and easily a perfectionist runs the risk of feeling down, blue, and depressed.

Learning more of perfectionist's beliefs, we can conclude this concept of perfectionism: if self-esteem is based primarily on external standards, this can lead to vulnerability and sensitivity to the opinions and criticisms of others. In attempting to protect him from such criticism, perfectionists may decide: being perfect is a defense and protection and the only way of existence.

At first glance maybe this seem beneficial and harmless, but it's not.

Writing on perfectionism I would like to clarify the definition of perfectionism. Perfectionism is not a healthy pursuit of excellence, therefore do not mix healthy goal setting with perfectionism. They are not the same! As someone said: the healthy striver has drive, while the perfectionist is driven!

It's hard to distinguish motivation for healthy achievement from unhealthy perfectionism. Especially in the western society there are so many myths on perfectionism, which makes everything more complicated to understand. For the benefits of a friend of mine and many others perfectionists I will explore some of the very common myths.

First myth is: perfection leads to success! True or false?

False: perfectionism does not lead to success despite that some perfectionists are very successful or more successful than non-perfectionists. According to psychologists there is evidence: with the same level of abilities, skills and intellect, perfectionists are less successful than their counterparts. Believe it or not, but it is true.

Who is a procrastinator and who misses the deadlines: perfectionist or non-perfectionist?

If your guess is perfectionist—you are right. Basically, perfectionists are, so called, "all-or-nothing" thinkers, meaning that a perfectionist sees any event as either good or bad, with nothing between these extremes. Such thinking leads to procrastination.

I have heard another statement: a perfectionist is ready to overcome any difficulties and obstacles just to reach his goal.

Unfortunately, that's just another myth! Contrary to the myth, a perfectionist is very vulnerable to any obstruction. Why is it so? Simply, because a perfectionist's centre of attention is always the result, not the process of reaching the goal itself! As a part of the team, perfectionist will be the very first member who will sabotage the project! Don't forget, a perfectionist is driven by low self-esteem.

What's the difference between great achievers and a perfectionist?

In one sentence: the great achievers will accept mistakes, failures, problems, and imperfections, as part of being human: a perfectionist won't!

I don't want to leave you with the wrong impression that perfectionists are "bad people". No, they are not. That personality has positive aspects, too. A positive aspect is that perfectionism can provide the driving energy, which leads to great achievement. But, if a perfectionist refuses to live with anything less than ideal, and if he is never satisfied, he is in trouble.

This attitude set in motion a vicious cycle. First, perfectionists set unreachable goals. Secondly, they fail to meet these goals, because the goals are impossible. Third, the constant pressure to achieve perfection reduces productivity and effectiveness. Fourth, this cycle leads perfectionists to be self-critical and self-blaming which results in lower self-esteem. They think people are just waiting to catch them in their imperfections. This may lead to further anxiety and depression.

Because of this cycle, perfectionists face the difficulty in getting close to other people and therefore, have less satisfactory personal relationships. Perfectionists have a hard time accepting friendship and love from others.

What can a perfectionist do to change himself?

The first step is: he must realize that perfectionism is an undesirable behavior, an illusion, not a real state of being. Then the person can change his way of thinking, by changing his mental attitude first, making him realize that the world will not end because he is not perfect.

The next step is to change these self defeating thoughts and behaviors which are the fuel for perfectionism. If a perfectionist is able to focus on doing and enjoying the task, to focus on an activity, not just on the result, then the person will be able to overcome his imperfection. A perfectionist needs support from people who will give him positive reinforcement for any positive change, no matter how small or slight it is.

As for any other fear, the perfectionist should confront the fear of failure and imperfection by asking himself: what am I afraid of?

What's so wrong by making mistakes? What is the worst thing that could happen?

They need to learn how to gain satisfaction from their achievements and how to learn from their mistakes seeing failure for what it really is: an opportunity to discover that future success lies in another tactics or direction.

The biggest challenge for a perfectionist, and not only for him, but for many others characters, is how to deal with a criticism.

Nobody wants to make mistakes, nobody wants to be a loser and everyone wants to be successful. I have no problem with that. I have a problem when people see criticism as a personal attack.

Criticism is a tragedy for a perfectionist. If someone criticizes him for making a mistake, a perfectionist cannot acknowledge the mistake and assert his right to make mistakes.

40

Self-Acceptance

Acceptance

Sometimes, when we are down, we worry too much, and we don't know what to do. We don't know how to cope with problems. Sometimes we have no chance to change anything. We feel that everything in our life is out of our control, out of our own power. We don't know how to cope with uncertainty and overwhelming challenges. We are stuck, not knowing where to go and what to do. How do we deal with such a situation? How do we cope?

There is way out of the blues! Our mental response is a very powerful tool. If we cannot change something, we can change the way we think about it. Understanding what can be done and what can't be done is the only right way to deal with adversity. We have a choice. There is always a choice. A choice to accept reality and uncertainty, or a choice to sit down and worry forever.

We are not able to control everything. The only thing that we can control is our reaction! Our response to what happens to us makes the difference. Don't deny reality. Instead, turn denial into acceptance. Let reality be reality. Accept, hope and cope!

Acceptance is similar to managing stress. Both affect our body and mind. Accepting reality is the right solution and the right choice. Do you know why? Because emotions don't have anything to do with our will. What can you do with emotions? You can accept them, experience them and express them. By doing that, we will expend a lot of energy. But acceptance releases energy.

I will explain: Whenever we worry, we use a lot of energy. Actually we lose energy. But when we accept reality, we regain our energy back. We really need energy to deal with situations; we need energy to survive. When we accept challenges, we save energy and protect ourselves from being sick by worrying.

Acceptance gives us a "feeling" of dealing with the situation. We get control over our life. Acceptance means: I don't need to fight. I will accept those things I can't change and get to work on those I can. I will accept whatever comes to me on my way through life. I am strong and prepared to understand that life is beautiful, in spite of all challenges. I am in charge of my own life. I am mature!

Acceptance is a source of power and serenity. Acceptance is not apathy! By accepting reality, we are taking responsibility for our life. When accepting reality we are gaining—not loosing. Acceptance is a skill that can save our life. Do not forget to accept and love yourself first. Everything starts with you first! As a coping technique, acceptance is not always welcome in Western society! Our society teaches us: Go and fight for it! Do not give up! You can do it! It's worth fighting for.

I have no problem with all those statements. I only have a problem with one thing: When should we use this fighting strategy? Who is going to tell us when to fight and when not to fight and accept? Use the Serenity Prayer as guidance: "God grant me the serenity to accept the things I cannot change, the courage to change the things I can, and the wisdom to know the difference". Our inner wisdom will tell us what to choose and what to do.

41

The Mind-Body Connection

From my personal point of view, generally speaking, people believe in the mind/body connection, but actually don't know how it works, which is not a bad thing. The bad thing is that only 30% of the attendants believe in the possibility of changing their mental approach. In everyday life, 70% of these people strongly believe in the statement that they cannot change their mental nature, which is incorrect. How wrong they are!

If you belong to that 70% of people who don't believe in changing their mental approach, please take a little time and read this article. Maybe you will change your way of thinking.

Now, I may have a hard time to convince you in believing in the neural/immune connection.

There is no doubt that the state of one's mind influences health and plays a huge role in physical illness, making us sick, helping us to recovery, or enabling us to live well. We have known this much from the time of the ancient Greeks. Or, more accurately, we knew it, but we didn't use it for a long time.

Alas!

To continue in the same vein, I'll give you the next fact: the human brain and the human immune system work together, signalling to each other along the same pathways. Now, you know why one's state of mind influences one's health.

For 60% of my audience, I need to explain that communication between the brain and the body is by chemicals, communicating on the molecular level. This is a two way route. Chemicals, produced by the brain, send signals to the body (immune system) and at the same time, chemicals from the immune system communicate with the brain. The same signals affect behavior and stress response.

This is a pure biochemical connection.

How does it work? Have you ever heard about neuro-transmitters? I am sure that you have, but I am going to repeat the definition.

Neuro-transmitters are chemicals, often amino acids, peptides or mono amides, which regulate signals between a neuron and another cell. Some of the most "popular" neurotransmitters are: acetylcholine, norepinephrine, dopamine, serotonin and glycine.

Any disturbance of communication between the brain and the immune system results in diseases. It could be auto-immune, inflammatory or infectious disease or it could be mood disorder. Personally, I was really impressed to learn that our state of mind can influence how well we resist against infectious/inflammatory diseases. Not only that, but our recovery depends on our state of mind. It is easy to see how impressive our mind's work is.

For many years we have known about interactions between the mind (nervous system) and the body (immune system) along with the effects of these interactions on diseases. It's a proven fact that the immune system is a target of signals from the brain and the endocrine system. Therefore, our experience, behavior, way of thinking and believing has a huge impact on the body and vice versa.

In essence, our immune system is listening to our mental talk.

When we are happy, our body is happy. When we are angry, our entire body is angry. There are messengers that literally transmit happiness, joy, and positive feelings, and there are messengers that transmit fear, stress, anxiety, and worry.

Next time, when you are under stress or are angry or worry too much, think about it. Stress hormones can change immune cell behavior and the activity of the immune system. As we know, this is a two-way street: our behavior can change immune functions and immune response can modulate our behavior.

As human beings we have a built-in tendency to resist change, regardless of if it's good or bad. We called it homeostasis or equilibrium and this is a natural system that wants to maintain things as they are. Our body responds to any threat to disturb our mental, physical, or emotional balance. Any threat to homeostasis is a kind of stress. Body reaction comes instinctively, automatically, and spontaneously with commands from our autonomic nervous system (the brain).

If you believe that only bad things are stress creators, think again.

Getting married or playing a game of tennis are stress creators causing the same response from our mind/body connection as loosing a job or money.

I don't blame people who don't believe in the mind/body connection. For many years, even scientific authorities were very skeptical. Actually, this is very understandable. The scientific approach depends on measurable evidence, such as abnormality of anatomy or physiology or any other visible evidence.

Now, we have molecular and pharmacological tools in our hands, including neuro-imaging, with which to observe the living human brain with the nerve cells' function. We can "see" biochemistry at work, or the nerve chemicals, including the electrical activity in the brain. Measurable proof is there and we can see it and believe it. Imbalance in neuro-transmitters is real and measurable and results in disease caused by emotions. We can observe and explore sick emotions. Isn't it amazing?

My intention in writing this article is to explain how strong the connection between our emotions (mind) and our body (immune system) is and how important it is to take care of our way of thinking. The failure to stop being an obsessive "what if" thinker, or a depressed, angry or anxious person, leads to chronic tension in our mind and makes us really physically sick.

When we are loving and thankful people, with no jealousy and resentment, our own mind will keep us well. Therefore, control your mood and behavior, slow down, your everyday rhythm, exercise at least five times per week and find an engrossing hobby. Relax your mind by meditation, yoga, or tai chi and your body will be thankful to you and reward you with good health.

42

What Makes us Happy and Why?

Happiness has always been seen as too vague as a concept. In the past 10-15 years, researchers have been trying to identify the factors that contribute to happiness. I wrote this article about happiness for the following reasons:

1. To learn more what happiness is about
2. To better understand what the causes of happiness are
3. To explore what contributes to happiness and a satisfying life
4. Clarify what is the purpose of happiness

I will be very happy if I succeed in providing an explanation for all the above.

Dr. Martin Seligman is the positive psychologist of the University of Pennsylvania who believes: it is possible to lift our biological set range of happiness, at least to some extent, if we work at it. His effort and the effort of his colleagues are to create a science of higher happiness, and a program to help people achieve it.

What is happiness for you?

Do you believe that the only form of happiness is pleasure? If you do, you generally pursue a media creation of happiness. You are watching too many Hollywood's movies!

I know you will just feel good temporarily. Pleasure will come only from what you have done to earn it. Please read what Nietzsche had to say:

"I slept and I dreamed that life is pleasure

I woke and I saw that it is duty

I worked and I realized that duty is pleasure."

To truly feel happy, we must have a goal, a point of destination we consider worthy of our effort which will satisfy us first, and make our life worthwhile. We need to build our own idea of critical thinking, love, kindness, and mindfulness. We need to live our life with enthusiasm, optimism, and morality. Only after reaching all these premises will we be a happy person. For reaching the higher forms of happiness - achieving satisfaction and contentment – we require taking paths leading to a meaningful life - a life where, through having goals, we will find fulfillment.

The question is: what makes us happy?

Make your own list of what makes you happy, and then compare it with the list made by scientists.

Happiness researchers have been monitoring people's life satisfaction for decades.

Most of the experts agree with the following conclusions:

1. Wealth and fortune do not contribute to happiness. There is a lot of evidence that being richer isn't making us happier, which is fair! The research suggests that once you have shelter or a modest home, basic food, and clothes, then extra money does not seem to make people much happier.

Now we have evidence: we can be happy without being rich, therefore no more excuses for being unhappy because you don't have a lot of money. According to many statistics, the standard of living in many countries has increased dramatically! I am not sure that's true for everyone, but let's accept it as a scientific fact!

If you ask Professor Daniel Kahneman of the University of Princeton, his answer is: "Standard of living has increased dramatically and happiness has increased not at all, and in some cases has diminished slightly."

Despite all the massive increase in wealth, our levels of happiness have not increased. We know the reason: it is our intention to adapt to pleasure. For example, buying a new car or purchasing a new home can give us a quick feeling of pleasure and at the same time can quickly wear off. Those kinds of pleasures have limitations and they gradually lose their power.

Pretty dark statement from the scientific point of view, isn't it?

2. Health, family and friends are the most important factors for our happiness. If you are a healthy person in relatively good shape, with a good family, and personal relationships, consider yourself a happy and a lucky person. Keep your marriage or relationship in good condition; marriage adds an average seven years to the life of a man and something like four for a woman. Happy people have a lot of friends, and they make very close friendships, too.

Just as a reminder: as stress can trigger ill health, friendship and happiness can have a protective effect. Now we know that our brain controls many of the mechanisms in our bodies which are responsible for diseases. What we learn from positive psychology is: friendship has a much bigger effect on happiness than a typical person's income. This is one more reason to believe that we can be happy despite having to struggle with a difficult financial situation. At this moment scientists cannot prove causation; whether, for example, people are healthy because they are happy, or whether people are happy because they are healthy.

3. Having goals and a meaningful life, a belief in something bigger than us—from religion, spirituality or a philosophy of life is crucial for our happiness. Finding meaning in life is like finding a gold mine. Dig it and you will find your lost goals and your lost happiness. With meaning and goals in your life, you will be always on track.

The theory sounds good, but what's the reality? The question is: whether we can actually use our knowledge of what makes us happy to lift our levels of happiness permanently? It's a very hot question for psychologists!

We need to accept the reality: life is not always all about happiness. Unhappiness is a part of life, too. Life is unpredictable with no guarantee for happiness. The mind rises and falls and illness can shift happiness into sadness. If you expect to be happy all the time you are making an unrealistic goal. The best you can do is to make an effort and learn what makes you a happy person. Also, not everything is in our hands. Science also came to the conclusion that one's happiness is genetically determined, and depends also on life's circumstances and personality. You don't have to be genetically predisposed to happiness to succeed, but you need to understand and train your mind to shift emotions from sadness to happiness, and how to pay attention to upsetting emotions.

Is there any room for criticism of the movement? Yes, many psychologists are critical!

But whatever is your conclusion about "power of happiness", don't forget one thing here: each blue day has a negative impact on health and life satisfaction in all of us. Cheerfulness has scientifically proven positive effects. We have the capacity to enhance our well-being by finding things that will make our lives more satisfying. It's our obligation to apply "that duty is pleasure". Happiness seems to have almost magical properties, which isn't easy to prove. But science suggests it leads to long life, health, resilience, and good performance.

Did I answer all your questions about happiness? Perhaps not, but I believe I did explain some very basic knowledge about positive psychology.

If you still worry about happiness, I know you live in a satisfying environment! Do you know why? Researchers know and agree: poor people or societies have no time to think about happiness. They need to fulfill their basic needs for food and shelter and therefore there is no time for thoughts about happiness. During catastrophic times, people do not talk about happiness, they talk about survival.

When people or societies do not have to worry about poverty or tragedy – they worry about happiness.

43

Workaholism

By definition, workaholism is an obsessive need to work, or compulsiveness (obsession) about working, akin to obsessive compulsive disorder. Workaholism is a progressive disease, and the most socially accepted addiction in modern society! Our society is pushing us more and more towards workaholism and at the same time asking us not to be addicted to alcohol or drugs!

On the contrary, very often workaholism goes hand in hand with alcoholism and drug abuse. If you believe that workaholism is associated with a paying job, you are incorrect, for it can also be associated with people who excessively practice sports, hobbies, fitness, housework or volunteering. Apparently, a person who suffers from workaholism is a workaholic, coined from "work" + "aholic", meaning addicted to something. Workaholic is a person who works a lot of the time, for very long hours, and has difficulty when not working.

At the very beginning of this chapter I need to clarify that the term workaholic is very often used inaccurately, to describe an energetic person who devotes a lot of time to work. Simply, it's not true. If that person has good relations with his family, co-workers and friends, takes pleasure on a regular basis, knows how to rest well, and refuses to work on weekends from home or at work, that person is not a workaholic. That person is a hard working person, not a workaholic. Here, I am not writing about hard working people, I am writing about workaholism and a workaholic person. In our everyday life, it is not so easy to recognize and understand a workaholic person. To recognize someone who is a workaholic is not so easy because of many misconceptions about workaholism. It may take a long time to understand that.

In this chapter I am going to make this addiction a little bit more understandable. Yes, workaholism is an addiction and a disease, and may be pleasurable to the victim, but is still addiction. It may be burdensome and troubling with harmful social behavior, and like all other addictive diseases, it is progressive. Once workaholism sets in, it progresses through stages similar to those in alcoholism and drug addiction. Like alcoholism, workaholism can have a detrimental effect on the spouse and children of the workaholic person. Since this is a progressive disease, ultimately the workaholic becomes more driven until he hits bottom. The bottom may come in the form of a serious health problem or an ultimatum from a partner, an employer, or a friend.

The philosophy of workaholism is very difficult to explain, since people always try to accuse you that you are wrong, lazy, old fashioned, uneducated or unambitious! I have personal experience with this misunderstanding when I brought up the subject of workaholism, and I had a hard time clarifying my stand. I would be curious to know your position on workaholism, after reading this article. The reality is that everyone needs to understand the real meaning of workaholism, with no prejudice or misconceptions, accepting the fact that every illness needs to be treated as soon as possible. If you still are wondering why workaholism is an illness, then you need to realize that work obsession is only the outward manifestation of the inner emotional disturbance. A workaholic is really a sick person, regardless if he (she) is aware of it or not.

Many people believe that our modern, western society makes many people workaholic, intentionally or not. Workaholics are praised and often promoted at work for being responsible and hard-working, or they may even be employed by a company that encourages workaholism. Unfortunately, many times the company uses praise and promotion to encourage the workaholic person to work harder, which can lead, in some cases, to addiction. Who is paying the price?

You bet, workaholics have to pay an enormous price.

What is the reason for workaholism? There are so many reasons, but some of the main ones are: competition among workers, a desire to show loyalty to the company, tight family budget, and constant demands from management and current corporate culture, which is a monumental obstacle. How to describe the characteristics of a workaholic personality?

The workaholic person is a perfectionist, who will not accept mistakes that are a part of being human, and feels the need to get more tasks done before he can feel good about himself. It's very difficult for a workaholic to relax, often feeling that he must complete certain tasks.

A workaholic believes that he is the only person capable of performing their work. His interpretation is: I am the only one who is capable of doing that task! Wrong! The world will not collapse if he doesn't work.

Workaholics overschedule their lives with unnecessary activities, and usually they do not necessarily love their work, weird but true. The problem with the workaholic people is that they can never get enough praise, money, or get enough accomplishment to truly feel good about themselves. Their sense of self-esteem is based largely on perceptions of how others judge their performance at work, and in other areas of their lives.

The problem with workaholic people is huge; they neglect their health, their relationships, and their spirituality; seeing everything as work-related. Very often the workaholic person will procrastinate, postponing vacations and rest. Perhaps others will feel fear, depression, anxiety, and loneliness. They do not often experience true serenity. With an obsessive desire to understand everything in their lives, which is an impossible task, they cannot allow themselves to experience emotions that they might not understand, fearing loss of control. They have the illusion that people will like them more if they appear more competent than they actually are. Here we are at the main point.

Generally speaking, workaholics are hurting on the inside, and that is the main cause of workaholism. They are not happy and satisfied people!

Everyone needs balance in life, but workaholics deny the enjoyment of a balanced and varied life, and they are concerned only with image. They think looking busy will make people think that they are important, but inside they feel the opposite. All these characteristics of workaholics are actually ways how the workaholic person copes with the pain of having lost the sense of being and of not feeling good enough about themselves. They keep busy to blot out their feelings, enjoying the adrenaline highs that come from intensity and rushing to meet work deadlines.

Workaholism is harmful and is a risky business for the human body. Overworked people lose sleep, eat poorly, and survive on caffeine and cigarettes. The legacy of long days and skipped vacations has a price tag; worker attrition, loss of productivity, illness, injury, and damaged relationships. Long hours can strain the body system and even the mind. Such long hours inevitably take their toll. The accumulation of stress at work and symptoms of arteriosclerosis and mental difficulties are often the result of overwork. We need to remember that hard work is healthy but overwork and workaholism can be "a gun to the head."

Recovery from workaholism is possible. It's a lifelong process that includes a big help from the workaholic person himself, his family, friends, and help from the most important - the professionals.

The process of recovery begins by being sincere to yourself, expressing your love to yourself! The workaholic, as everyone else, needs to understand and love himself first.

Everything else comes after that.

He needs a quiet time only for himself with his mind focusing on his mind/body connection. He needs to be busy with "being" not with "doing."

The workaholic needs to learn to take vacations and use weekend getaways each and every weekend. He needs to rediscover his private and family life, and improve his social life. It is a huge challenge for him! Some forms of professional help are necessary for recovery.

Honestly, I am not sure how to close this topic on workaholism.

Waiting for "my inspiration" I found an excellent speech made by Anna Qunidlen, who is a novelist. Her work deals with human nature.

With parts from Anna's speech, I will close this article hoping that you learn more about this addiction called workaholism!

"Don't ever confuse the two, your life and your work. The second is only part of the first. You cannot be really good at your work if your work is all you are. No man ever said on his deathbed I wish I had spent more time at the office. People do not talk about the soul very much anymore. It is so much easier to write a resume than to craft a spirit. But a resume is a cold comfort on a winter night or when you are sad, broke, lonely, or sick.

Enjoy your entire life. Not just your life at the desk. Not just the life of your mind, but the life of your heart. No just your bank account but your soul. Get a life... a real life not a manic pursuit of the next promotion, the bigger paycheck, the larger house. Do you think you'd care so very much about those things if you had an aneurysm one afternoon?

Get a life in which you notice the smell of salt water.... a life in which you stop and watch... a life in which you are not alone... a life in which you are generous. Find people you love and who love you. Learn to look at all the good in the world and try to give some of it back. Learn to be happy."

44

Your Perception is Everything

How we become aware of success, failure, happiness, friendships, love, and everything else is just a perception. It is how we perceive failure or defeat, and what we do with it, that makes all the difference. Actually, perception is our personal opinion or our point of view about any particular event. Of course, the event is a fact, not imagination, but at the same time there is a very personal view coloring the event. We really need to accept the truth about our emotions and perceptions: our thoughts and attitudes create our emotions—not the external events!

Our own perception depends on many things. These include our attitude, which, in turn, includes self-acceptance, self-confidence, self-respect and other things. Because your mental structure is different from my mental structure we see the same situation differently. The same pleasant or unpleasant episode is not the same for you and me. You choose your own perception and the consequences are yours, not mine.

Is it clear? If not, may I remind you about cognitive distortion? Cognitive distortion simply means that our thoughts and our way of thinking sometimes misrepresent the facts. Our own mental filter chooses how we feel. This filter will pick up any detail to prove that things are as we perceive them-negative or positive--but mostly negative! Sounds strange but any kind of behavior is a conscious choice. I didn't choose for my friend to be angry or upset. I am sorry if I am unkind but this is a reality that my friend doesn't want to see and understand. It was his attitude, his perception, of this "disturbing event" that led him to his behavior.

It is necessary to understand that sometimes the next day we will see the same event differently. How is it possible? The next day we are wearing a different "pair of eyeglasses." That is, a different mental filter. Yes, we are very fashion-conscious in that respect--we change our mental filter every time we process our thoughts. Now you know why some days are "so bad, boring and disturbing" for you. Your emotions-fear, anger, anxiety and guilt are a direct result of your mental processing system that day. Don't blame the weather, the event, the company, the other person or the government.

Our emotions are an indirect response to our environment, based on our inner thought processes. When our thoughts are in conflict with one another--cognitive distortions—or with reality, they will produce a sensation we will call emotion. All emotions are actually a result of an inappropriate response to external events. Actually, they are cognitive distortions.

If you see my friend around, tell him to change his "pair of glasses". He will feel better. I, however, was not able to do it. I couldn't explain to him that he feels so negative and angry because he assumed things were otherwise than they really were.

We all need to accept one thing: our emotions follow our thoughts. It took me a long time to logically understand that the only person who is in charge of my feelings and emotions is me. I am responsible for my "pair of eyeglasses". Whenever I start to feel inappropriately "emotional," I ask myself: What kind of mental filter is in my mind today? Where is the twisted thinking?

The more depressed or miserable I feel, the surer I am the more twisted my thinking is! In the absence of mental distortion

I cannot experience my anger, fear, anxiety or depression. What about you?

Persevering from a different perspective is a very healthy way of living. We will save a lot of energy and do our nerves a favour if we can wear the appropriate "pair of eyeglasses". And we won't save just energy - maybe you can save your marriage, or friendship, or even a job!

Next time when you or someone else says, "I am sorry, that's my mood," don't be afraid to say, "Yes, I understand that, but you can change it. You have an obligation to feel better about yourself."

45

A Guide for Creative Thinking

Einstein once said, "Every child is born a genius." But the reason why most people do not function at genius levels is because they are not aware of how creative and smart they really are.

I call it the "Schwarzenegger effect." No one would look at a person such as Arnold Schwarzenegger and think how lucky he is to have been born with such tremendous muscles. Everyone knows that he, and people like him, have worked many thousands of hours to build up their bodies so they can compete and win in bodybuilding competitions. Your creative capabilities are just the same. They actually grow as they are used.

But you don't need to spend thousands of hours to increase your creative-thinking abilities. By practicing a few simple exercises and applications, you can start your creative juices flowing, and you may even amaze yourself at the quality and quantity of good ideas that you come up with.

Let's start off with the definition of creativity. In my estimation, after years of research on this subject, the very best definition of creativity is, simply, "improvement." You don't have to be a rocket scientist or an artist in order to be creative. All you have to do is develop the ability to improve your situation, wherever you are and whatever you are doing. All great fortunes were started with ideas for improving something in some way. In fact, an improvement needs to be only 10 percent new or different to launch you on the way to fame and riches.

It has been estimated that each year, driving to and from work, the average person has about four ideas for improvement, any one of which could make him or her a millionaire. The problem is not that you don't have the ideas you need to accomplish anything you want but, rather, that you fail to act on those ideas. Most people dismiss their own ideas because they think that those ideas cannot be very valuable if they were the ones who thought of them.

Thomas Edison, arguably the most successful creative genius in human history, once said that creativity is 99 percent perspiration and only 1 percent inspiration. Extensive research on creativity tends to bear him out.

There are four generally accepted parts of the creative process: There is preparation, where much of the work is done. There is cerebration or rumination, where you turn the matter over to your subconscious mind. There is realization, where the idea or ideas come to you. And finally, there is application, where you work out the creative idea and turn it into something worthwhile. Of the four, preparation seems to be the most important, and it involves gathering the right data and asking the right questions.

Your success in life will be determined largely by the quantity of ideas that you generate. It seems that the quality of ideas is secondary to the quantity and that if you have enough ideas, one or more of them will turn out to be prizewinners.

You can begin building your creative muscles with focused questions. Some that you might think of are the following: What are we trying to do? How are we trying to do it? What are our assumptions? What if our assumptions are wrong?

All improvements begin with questioning the current, existing circumstances. If you are not making progress for any reason, stop and think, and begin asking yourself the hard questions that will stimulate your mind to consider other possibilities.

When they were doing the research to land a man on the moon, scientists were stumped for months and even years. They could not figure how to send a rocket to the moon with enough fuel to land on the moon, blast off, break the moon's gravity and come back to earth. The problem was that if the rocket had that much fuel to start with, it would be too heavy to take off from the earth in the first place. Finally, they began to question the assumption that the lunar rocket ship had to land on the moon. When they questioned that assumption, the scientists concluded that a main rocket could orbit around the moon while a smaller module dropped to the surface of the moon and then rejoined the orbiting rocket for the trip back to earth. The mental logjam was broken, and the rest is history.

Asking focused questions-hard questions that penetrate to the core of the matter-is the real art of the creative person. The next step is to have the courage to deal with all the possible answers. Once you have come up with a possible solution, ask yourself, "What else could be the solution?" If your current method of operation were completely wrong, what would be your backup plan? What else would you or could you do? What if your current procedure or plan turned out to be a complete failure? Then what would you do? And what would you do after that? All of those questions will force you to think further and come up with better answers.

The second way to build your mental muscles is with intensely desired goals. The more you want something and the clearer you are about it, the more likely it is that you will generate ideas that will help you to move toward it. That is why the need for clearly written goals and plans for their accomplishment is repeated over and over. Any intense emotion, such as desire, stimulates creativity and ideas to fulfill that desire. And the more you write down your goals and plans, and review them, the more likely it is that you will see all kinds of possibilities for achieving those goals.

The third generator of creative-thinking muscles is a pressing problem. A good question to ask is "What are the three biggest problems that I am facing in my life today?" Write the answer to this question quickly, in less than 30 seconds. When you write the answer to a question in less than 30 seconds, your subconscious mind will sort out all extraneous answers and give you the three most important ones.

When you have your three most pressing problems, ask yourself, "What is the worst possible thing that can happen as a result of each of these problems?" Then ask yourself, "What are all the things that I can do, right now, to alleviate each problem?" If you have a problem that is worrying you for any reason, think about what you could do immediately to begin alleviating that concern. This is a prime use of your creative powers.

So a key to success in creative thinking is clarity. Take the time to think through, discuss, and ask questions that help you to clarify exactly what you are trying to accomplish and exactly what problems you are facing at the present moment. Just as fuzzy thinking leads to fuzzy answers, clear thinking leads to clear answers.

A second key is concentration. Put everything else aside, and concentrate single-mindedly on focusing all your mental powers on solving one single problem, overcoming one particular obstacle or achieving one important goal. The ability to concentrate on a single subject without diversion or distraction is a hallmark of the superior thinker.

A third key is an open mind. The average person tends to be rigid and fixed in his thinking about getting from where he is to where he wants to go. The creative thinker, however, tends to remain very flexible and open to a variety of ways of approaching the problem. The average person has a tendency to leap to conclusions and determine that there is only one way to achieve a particular goal. The superior thinker, on the other hand, tends to be more patient and willing to consider a variety of options before moving toward a conclusion.

There is one other creative concept that can be very helpful when it is used in combination with what we have already discussed, and it is called the "limiting step."

Between you and any goal that you want to achieve or any problem that you want to solve, there is almost invariably a limiting step or a "choke point" that determines the speed with which you move from where you are to your destination. This limiting step may be another person, a particular obstacle, a specific difficulty, or even a lack of some information or skill. Invariably, there is a particular factor that determines how fast you get there. Your job is to think about it and decide what it is, and then go to work to remove it.

For example, if you are in sales, your limiting step may be the number of prospects you have. If this is the case, then your job is to do everything possible and to use all your creative capacities to increase your number of prospects until it is no longer a problem. Then, of course, there will be another limiting step, and your job is to go to work on that.

If you have a business, your limiting step may be the number of qualified people who are responding to your advertising. If this is the choke point that hinders the amount you sell and the speed at which your company grows, it is necessary for you to concentrate your mental powers on relieving that bottleneck. You must concentrate the very best thinking abilities of yourself and others on increasing the number of qualified prospects that your advertising and promotional efforts attract.

In relationships and misunderstandings between people, there is almost invariably a sticking point or subject area that needs to be resolved in order to bring about harmony again. Your job is, first, to identify this limiting step and then, second, to find a way to alleviate the difficulty to the satisfaction of everyone involved.

You are a genius, and you were born with the potential for exceptional creativity. But creative abilities are latent. They are like muscles that grow with use. You can increase your creative powers by using them, over and over, in every situation, deliberately and specifically, until creativity and a creative response to life is as natural to you as breathing in and out is. There are very few things that you can do that can have a more powerful positive impact on your entire life than becoming excellent in creative thinking. And you can if you think you can.

46

Accessing Your Inner Guidance

We know that the body has a natural bias toward health and energy. It's designed to last for 100 years with proper care and maintenance. When something goes wrong with any part of our body, we experience it in the form of pain or discomfort of some kind.

We know that when our body is not functioning smoothly and painlessly, something is wrong, and we take action to correct it. We go to a doctor; we take pills; we undergo physical therapy, massage or treatment. We know that if we ignore pain or discomfort for any period of time, it could lead to something more serious.

Every disease or ailment, whether it be cancer, diabetes, arthritis, high blood pressure or something else, has a series of warning signs. In every case, when we experience an abnormality, we tend to move quickly to do something to get back to normal. Our physical feelings tell us when we're well, and they also tell us when we're unwell, and we tend to obey them if we want to live a long, healthy life.

In the same sense, nature also gives us a way to tell what's right for us and what's wrong for us in life. Just as nature gives us physical pain to guide us to doing or not doing things in the physical realm, nature gives us emotional pain to guide us toward doing or not doing things in the emotional or mental realm. The wonderful thing is that you're constructed so that if you simply listen carefully to yourself—to your mind, your body and your emotions—and follow the guidance you're given, you can dramatically enhance the quality of your life.

Just as the natural physical state is health and vitality, the natural emotional state is peace and happiness. Whenever you experience a deviation from peace and happiness, it's an indication that something is amiss. Something is wrong with what you're thinking, doing or saying. You're an incredibly complex organism, and your feelings of ease and unease, happiness and unhappiness, can be triggered by a myriad of factors. But the bottom line is that your feeling of inner happiness is the best indicator you could ever have to tell you what you should be doing more of and what you should be doing less of.

Unhappiness is to your life as pain is to your body. It's sent as a messenger to tell you that what you're doing is wrong for you. There are many reasons why people don't listen more closely to their feelings and, especially, why many people are reluctant to use their own happiness as the standard by which to judge the events in their lives. I've studied this subject for many years, and I think that there are three major myths about happiness that each of us believes to some degree.

The first myth about happiness is that it is not legitimate or correct for you to put your happiness ahead of everyone else's. Throughout my life, I've met people who have said that it is more important to make other people happy than it is to make yourself happy. Of course, that is nonsense.

Human beings are happiness-driven organisms. Everything we do in life is oriented toward maintaining and increasing our level of happiness. We are psychologically constructed so that it's impossible for us to be any other way without making ourselves mentally and emotionally ill. The fact is that you can't give away to anyone else what you don't have for yourself. Just as you can't give money to the poor if you don't have any, you can't make someone else happy if you yourself are miserable.

The very best way to assure the happiness of others is to be happy yourself and then to share your happiness with them. Suffering and self-sacrifice merely depress and discourage other people. If you want to make others happy, start by living the kind of life and doing the kind of things that make you happy.

The second myth, which is closely tied to the first myth, is the admonition that we're here to serve others rather than ourselves. Many poems and essays repeat that theme. They say that we've justified our life on this earth if we've made some other person happy on the way through. But as I've said before, making others happy goes hand in hand with making ourselves happy. It's through service to others that we achieve a sense of meaning and purpose in life. Only when we lose ourselves in doing something that we feel benefits someone other than ourselves do we experience transcendence, do we feel ourselves rising above the tedium of day-to-day activity. To paraphrase Robert Louis Stevenson, everybody makes his living by serving someone. And the key is to serve with joy and happiness.

The third myth about happiness is that someone else's definition of happiness is valid for you. Often, we feel a little uneasy if we're not happy doing something that someone else thinks should make us happy. Many people allow their parents to influence their choices of career and find themselves miserable as a result. They want to please their parents, they want to make them happy, but they're unable to experience any joy doing what they're doing.

Happiness in life is like a smorgasbord. If 100 people went to a smorgasbord and each put food on his plate in the quantity and mix that each felt would be most pleasing to him, every plate would be different. Even a husband and wife would go up to the smorgasbord and come back with plates that looked completely different. Happiness is the same way. It's composed of a great variety of ingredients, physical, mental, emotional and spiritual. Each person requires a particular combination of those ingredients to feel the very best about himself or herself.

And your mix is changing continually. If you went to the same smorgasbord every day for a year, you probably would come back with a different plateful of food each time. Each day—sometimes each hour—only you can tell what it takes to make you happy. Therefore, the only way to judge whether a job, a relationship, an investment, or any decision, is right for you is to get in touch with your feelings and listen to your heart.

In the play *Cyrano de Bergerac by* Edmond Rostand, there's a scene where someone asks Cyrano why he, as an incredible individualist, should refuse to compromise his ideals or principles for anyone. He replies with these classic words: "I long ago made the decision that in every area of life, I will choose the path of least resistance in this, that I will please at least myself in all things." That is one of the great lines in literature. To have the courage to please at least yourself in all things. Do what feels right for you, at the very minimum, and if it makes others happy as well, that's terrific. If it doesn't, you'll know that you have done the very best you could under the circumstances.

You're true to yourself only when you follow your inner light, when you listen to what Ralph Waldo Emerson called the "still, small voice within." You're being the very best person you can be only when you have the courage and the fortitude to allow your definition of happiness, whatever it may be, to be the guiding light of every part of your life. Whenever you feel stressed, anxious, worried or uneasy about any part of your life, it's nature's way of telling you that something is wrong. It's a message that there's something that you need to address or deal with. There's something that you need to do more or less of. There's something that you need to get into or out of. Very often, you'll suffer from what has been called "divine discontent." You'll feel fidgety and uneasy for a reason or reasons that are unclear to you. You'll be dissatisfied with the status quo. Sometimes, you'll be unable to sleep. Sometimes, you'll be angry or irritable. Very often, you'll get upset with things that have nothing to do with the real issue. You'll have a deep inner sense that something isn't as it should be, and you'll often feel like a fish on a hook, wriggling and squirming emotionally to get free.

And that is a good thing. Divine discontent always comes before a positive life change. If you were perfectly satisfied, you would never take any action to improve or change your circumstances. Only when you're dissatisfied for some reason do you have the inner motivation to engage in the outer behaviors that lead you onward and upward.

You've heard of Murphy's Law, which says that whatever can go wrong will go wrong. Well, there's another law, which says that left to themselves, things have a tendency to go from bad to worse. When something is making you unhappy, for any reason, the situation will tend to get worse rather than better. So avoid the temptation to engage in denial, to pretend that nothing is wrong, to wish and hope and pray that, whatever it is, it will go away and you won't have to do anything. The fact is that it probably will get worse before it gets better and that ultimately you will need to face the situation and do something about it.

There's an old saying that you can't solve a problem on the level that you meet it. This means that wrestling with a challenge is usually fruitless and frustrating. For example, if two people who are in a relationship together are constantly fighting and negotiating and looking for some way to resolve their difficulties, they're attempting to solve the problem on the wrong level. Dealing with the problem on a higher level, those people would ask the question, "In terms of being happy, is this the right relationship for us in the first place?" As soon as you begin to use happiness as your measure of rightness, you begin to see a situation entirely differently. Many people work very hard and experience considerable frustration trying to do a particular job. However, in terms of their own happiness, the right answer might be to do something else, or to do what they're doing in a different place, or to do it with different people-or all three.

Following are a few questions for you to answer in this arena of happiness. Many people refuse to even consider these questions because they're afraid that if they do, they won't like the answers. But nevertheless, have the courage to clearly define your life in your own terms. Here are the questions; write them down at the top of a sheet of paper, and then write as many answers to each one as you possibly can.

The first question is: "What would it take for me to be perfectly happy?" Write down every single thing that you can imagine would be in your life if you were perfectly happy at this very moment. Write down things such as health, happiness, prosperity, loving relationships, inner peace, travel, car, clothes, homes, money, and so on. Let your mind run freely. Imagine that you have no limitations at all. Write everything down whether or not you think you have the capacity to acquire it or achieve it in the short term. Your first job is always to be clear about what it would take for you to have your ideal life.

The second question is a little tougher. Write down at the top of a page this question: "In what situations in my life, and with whom, am I not perfectly happy?" Force yourself to think about every part of your day, from morning to night, and write down every element that makes you unhappy or dissatisfied in any way. Remember, proper diagnosis is half the cure. Identifying the problematic situations is the first step to resolving them.

The third question will give you some important guidelines. Write down at the top of a sheet of paper these words: "In looking over my life, where and when have I been the happiest? Where was I, with whom was I, and what was I doing?"

By asking and answering those three questions, you begin to delve deeper and deeper into yourself and your feelings. You begin to accept your own happiness as a legitimate standard by which to evaluate everyone and everything in your life. You begin to develop the wisdom, the courage, and the foresight to organize your life in such a way that you become a much happier person.

Once you have the answers to those questions, think about what you can do, starting immediately, to begin creating the kind of life that you dream of. It may take you a week, a month or a year, but that doesn't matter. Every single thing you do that moves you closer to your vision of happiness will be rewarding in itself. You'll become a more positive and optimistic person. You'll feel more confident and more in charge of your life.

And now here's the most important exercise of all. It is from the advice of Dr. Gerald Jampolsky, who asks, "Do you want to be right, or do you want to be happy?" He recommends that you set peace of mind as your highest goal and that you select and organize around it all your other goals in life. You hold up each part of your life to this standard of peace of mind, and you either get into or get out of anything that adds to it or detracts from it.

The most important part in this process of getting in touch with your feelings is to begin to practice solitude on a regular basis. Solitude is the most powerful activity in which you can engage. Men and women who practice it correctly and on a regular basis never fail to be amazed at the difference it makes in their lives.

Most people have never practiced solitude. Most people have never sat down quietly by themselves for any period of time in their entire lives. Most people are so busy being busy, doing something-even watching television-that it's highly unusual for them to simply sit, deliberately, and do nothing. But as Catherine Ponder points out, "Men and women begin to become great when they begin to take time quietly by themselves, when they begin to practice solitude." And here's the method you can use.

To get the full benefit of your periods of solitude, you must sit quietly for at least 30 to 60 minutes at a time. If you haven't done it before, it will take the first 25 minutes or so for you to stop fidgeting and moving around. You'll almost have to hold yourself physically in your seat. You'll have an almost irresistible desire to get up and do something. But you must persist.

Solitude requires that you sit quietly, perfectly still, back and head erect, eyes open, without cigarettes, candy, writing materials, music or any interruptions whatsoever for at least 30 minutes. An hour is better.

Become completely relaxed, and breathe deeply. Just let your mind flow. Don't deliberately try to think about anything. The harder you "don't try," the more powerfully it works. After 20 or 25 minutes, you'll begin to feel deeply relaxed. You'll begin to experience a flow of energy coming into your mind and body. You'll have a tremendous sense of well-being. At this point, you'll be ready to get the full benefit of these moments of contemplation.

The incredible thing about solitude is that if it is done correctly, it works just about 100 percent of the time. While you're sitting there, a stream, a river, of ideas will flow through your mind. You'll think about countless subjects in an uncontrolled stream of consciousness. Your job is just to relax and listen to your inner voice. At a certain stage during your period of solitude, the answers to the most pressing difficulties facing you will emerge quietly and clearly, like a boat putting in gently to the side of a lake. The answer that you seek will come to you so clearly and it will feel so perfect that you'll experience a deep sense of gratitude and contentment. You may get several answers in one period of quiet sitting. But in any case, you'll get the answer to the most important situation facing you every single time.

When you arise from this period of quiet, you must do exactly what has come to you. It may involve dealing with a human situation. It may involve starting something or quitting something. Whatever it is, when you follow the guidance that you received in solitude, it will turn out to be exactly the right thing to do. Everything will be OK. And it will usually work out far better than you could have imagined. Just try it and see.

That brings us to the final point on getting in touch with your feelings: You must learn to trust yourself. You must learn to take time to listen to your emotions and your feelings as to what makes you happy or unhappy, as to what feels right or wrong. You must absolutely trust that what is right for you is the right thing to do. You must never compromise on what your inner voice tells you to do. You must never go against what you feel to be correct. You must develop the habit of listening to yourself and then acting on the guidance you receive.

When you listen to yourself and act on what you hear inside, you are setting out on the road to personal greatness.

47

Accessing Your Intuition

It has been said that men and women become great when they begin to listen to their inner voices. Your intuition is your direct connection with infinite intelligence. Intuition is so powerful that it has been studied and written about by the greatest men and women of history for thousands of years. When you begin to use it regularly and systematically, there is virtually nothing that you cannot accomplish.

Your intuition has often been called the "still small voice" within. You may experience your intuition as a gut-feeling, as an inner sense of what is right or wrong for you. Sometimes your intuition manifests itself as a hunch or an inspiration. Often it comes as a flash of insight. Your intuition leads you to new ideas, concepts and breakthroughs. Sometimes, an intuitive flash will enable you to see a situation completely differently and solve it on a completely different level. Einstein was referring to intuition when he said, "No problem can be solved on the same level at which you meet it."

In breakthrough thinking, we are taught to redefine a problem and take it to a higher level in order to find a solution for it. Since the more you do of what you're doing, the more you'll get of what you've got, trying to solve your current problem at your current level is often an exercise in frustration. You can unlock your intuition by using your imagination to think about your problem in a completely different way.

There are two major types of imagination that you use continually, both of which require the highest use of your intuitive powers. They are first, synthetic imagination and, second, creative imagination. Synthetic imagination is your ability to assemble existing pieces of knowledge and information into new forms. It is very much like taking all the pieces of a jigsaw puzzle, having a clear idea of the picture or goal that you want to accomplish and assembling them into a single piece.

This form of imagination is often called, "integrative intelligence." It is one of the highest forms of intelligence for success and achievement anywhere. Integrative intelligence is defined as your ability to integrate a large number of different pieces of information into a single precept for decision and action. It is your ability to recognize and sort many different facts and insights together, emphasizing some and discarding others, in the process of making the correct decision. This form of intelligence is extremely valuable in fast-moving, fluid situations that require your considering a large number of different pieces of information in making a decision.

It has been estimated that you need between 20,000 and 50,000 bits of information at your disposal to be really successful in any field of endeavor. We live in the information age, and knowledge is the raw material of production and value in this age. So the more different bits or "bytes" of information that you have, the more effective your integrative intelligence, or synthetic imagination, will be.

The people who rise to the top of any field of endeavour are invariably those who know more than others. In fact, the division in our society today is not between those who "have more" and "have less" but between those who "know more" and those who "know less." One of your jobs is to be continually gathering additional bits of practical and useful information so that you have plenty of different ideas and concepts to draw upon when you are wrestling with any problem or striving toward any goal. Your intuition then goes to work for you by helping you quickly sort out the relevant facts and giving you the answers you need when you need them.

The more ideas you expose yourself to, the greater the probability that the right idea will appear at the right time. When it does, your intuition will help you to recognize the idea and integrate it into everything else you are doing.

The second form of imagination is creative imagination. This is a higher form of imagination where intuition plays an even more important part. Creative imagination refers to your ability to come up with completely new and different ideas and concepts to solve your problems and achieve your goals. It is the highest form of imagination and is responsible for all the great breakthroughs in science, technology, art, music, literature, and medicine. The most successful men and women of all time have been those who have deliberately trained themselves to tap into their creative imagination on a regular basis. And so can you, if you learn how. Your creative imagination is the source of all hunches, inspirations, imagination, flashes of insight and new understandings of complex concepts. The cultivation and development of your creative imagination can enable you to make more progress in one or two years than the average person might make in ten or twenty. And your creativity, your intuitive sense is like a muscle. It grows with use. The more you practice with it and rely on it, the stronger it becomes and the faster it acts for you.

Men and women who have highly developed imaginations have often reached the point where they completely trust their intuition, their inner voices, to guide them in every situation. They never speak or act until they feel an inner urging to do so. They know that their intuition will always bring them exactly the right answer, at exactly the right time.

Your intuition is your direct pipeline to a form of intelligence that is completely beyond your conscious brain. It is accessed by your subconscious mind, which is controlled by the thoughts you think and the beliefs you hold in your conscious mind. The more you affirm and visualize your desired goals in your conscious mind, the more readily they are picked up by your subconscious mind and the more rapidly your intuition or creative imagination is triggered. Successful, effective, happy people are those who have gotten onto the beam of their own intuitive senses and who rely continuously on their inner guidance. And they seldom make mistakes.

In your lifetime, you have made a lot of decisions, some of them right and some of them wrong. But when your intuition tells you to do or to not do something, it is always correct. If you have ever gone against your intuition, your inner voice, haven't you regretted it? Wherever you have pushed aside that nagging inner feeling, hasn't it come back to haunt you? This is because your intuition is always correct. It always gives you exactly the right answer for you at any given time, and in any given situation. One of the smartest things that you can ever do is to listen carefully to your intuition and to postpone making a decision until you have an inner sense of what choices are correct.

You will often find that your intuition will urge you to either speak up or to remain silent in a social or business situation. Later, it will turn out that that was exactly the right thing to do. In retrospect, you will find that your intuitive learning has always been more accurate than anything that you could think of with your conscious mind.

All the great writers, composers, artists, and scientists have developed the habit of listening to their intuition. You have access to the same intuitive powers as the smartest men and women who ever lived.

By the way, research shows that men and women, tested separately, have intuitions that are equally accurate. They seem to come up with the same intuitive answers for complex problems and questions. Why is it, then, that women's intuition is more respected than men's? The answer is simple. Women listen to their intuition more, while men have a tendency to brush it aside.

When a woman says, "This situation doesn't feel right," she views this feeling as a valid and important assessment of whether the situation is right or wrong. Women are very respectful of their intuitive feelings and they generally refuse to go against them. Men will often put aside their intuitive leanings in favour of short-term advantage, only to pay the price later.

Perhaps the best method for stimulating your intuition is by learning to practice solitude on a regular basis. Throughout the ages, the greatest thinkers of all time have practiced solitude as a regular part of their work and life. They have taken time to be alone with themselves. They have gone off and sat quietly prior to any situation of importance. Most of the great thinkers of today use solitude as an essential tool in developing the creative insights and intuitions that often have the power to change our lives.

Most people have never practiced solitude because they wrongly believe that they have no time for it. However, one good idea that comes to you in the silence of solitude can save you a year of hard work. You cannot afford not to practice solitude on a regular basis. Here's how you do it.

First, find a place to sit where you can be completely alone, in silence, without interruptions. You want to avoid any activities that will disturb your reverie, such as eating, drinking, listening to music, and getting telephone calls. You can sit in your basement, your backyard, or on a park bench. The main objective is to be completely alone with yourself.

And second, force yourself to sit without moving for 60 minutes. The first 25 or 30 minutes will be excruciatingly difficult. You will have an irresistible urge to get up and walk around. But you must persist. You must force yourself to stay still.

After 25 or 30 minutes, a wonderful thing will happen. You will start to feel very good about yourself and your life. You will relax completely. Your mind will become calm and clear. You will feel energy flowing through your body. The situations and difficulties of your life will seem to fade away, and you will begin to get tremendous clarity on how to reach your goals.

At the end of your 60 minutes, get up and do exactly what your intuition told you to do. Don't worry about whether or not people will like it or approve of it. Just take the action, make the commitment, do the deed. You will find later that this was exactly the right thing to do.

Solitude requires no energy, no effort, no trying at all. It simply requires a state of relaxed awareness where you open your mind to infinite intelligence. And at the right moment, exactly the right answer you need will come to you, in exactly the right form.

You can overcome any obstacle, solve any problem or achieve any goal by tapping into the incredible powers of your mind and by trusting your intuition in everything you do. Once you begin to develop and use your intuition, you will become more alert, more aware, smarter and more effective in everything that you do. And your potential will begin to unfold at a speed that you cannot now imagine.

48

Becoming a Person of Integrity

Integrity is a value, like persistence, courage, and industriousness. Even more than that, it is the value that guarantees all the other values. You are a good person to the degree to which you live your life consistent with the highest values that you espouse. Integrity is the quality that locks in your values and causes you to live consistent with them.

Integrity is the foundation of character. And character development is one of the most important activities you can engage in. Working on your character means disciplining yourself to do more and more of those things that a thoroughly honest person would do, under all circumstances.

To be impeccably honest with others, you must first be impeccably honest with yourself. You must be true to yourself. You must be true to the very best that is in you, to the very best that you know. Only a person who is living consistent with his or her highest values and virtues is really living a life of integrity. And when you commit to living this kind of life, you will find yourself continually raising your own standards, continually refining your definition of integrity and honesty.

You can tell how high your level of integrity is by simply looking at the things you do in your day-to-day life. You can look at your reactions and responses to the inevitable ups and downs of life. You can observe the behaviors you typically engage in and you will then know the person you are.

The external manifestation of high integrity is high-quality work. A person who is totally honest with himself or herself will be someone who does, or strives to do, excellent work on every occasion. The totally honest person recognizes, sometimes unconsciously, that everything he or she does is a statement about who he or she really is as a person.

When you start a little earlier, work a little harder, stay a little later and concentrate on every detail, you are practicing integrity in your work. And whether you know it or not, your true level of integrity is apparent and obvious to everyone around you.

Perhaps the most important rule you will ever learn is that your life only becomes better when you become better.

All of life is lived from the inside out. At the very core of your personality lie your values about yourself and life in general. Your values determine the kind of person you really are. What you believe has defined your character and your personality. It is what you stand for, and what you won't stand for, that tells you and the world the kind of person you have become.

Ask yourself this question: What are your five most important values in life? Your answer will reveal an enormous amount about you. What would you pay for, sacrifice for, suffer for and even die for? What would you stand up for, or refuse to lie down for? What are the values that you hold most dear? Think these questions through carefully and, when you get a chance, write down your answers. Here's another way of asking that question. What men and women, living or dead, do you most admire? Once you pick three or four men or women, the next question is: Why do you admire them? What values, qualities, or virtues do they have that you respect and look up to? Can you articulate those qualities? What is a quality possessed by human beings in general that you most respect? This is the starting point for determining your values. The answers to these questions form the foundation of your character and your personality.

Once you have determined your five major values, you should now organize them in order of importance. What is your first, most important value? What is your second value? What is your third value? And so on. Ranking your values is one of the very best and fastest ways to define your character.

Remember, a higher order value will always take precedence over a lower order value. Whenever you are forced to choose between acting on one value or another, you always choose the value that is the highest on your own personal hierarchy.

Who you are, in your heart, is evidenced by what you do on a day-to-day basis, especially when you are pushed into a position where you have to make a choice between two values or alternatives. Ralph Waldo Emerson said, "Guard your integrity as a sacred thing." In study after study, the quality of integrity, or a person's adherence to values, ranks as the number one quality sought in every field. When it comes to determining whom they will do business with, customers rank the honesty of a salesperson as the most important single quality. Even if they feel that a salesperson's product, quality, and price is superior, customers will not buy from that salesperson if they feel that he or she is lacking in honesty and character.

Likewise, integrity is the number one quality of leadership. Integrity in leadership is expressed in terms of constancy and consistency. It is manifested in an absolute devotion to keeping one's word. The glue that holds all relationships together—including the relationship between the leader and the led—is trust, and trust is based on integrity.

Integrity is so important that functioning in our society would be impossible without it. We could not make even a simple purchase without a high level of confidence that the price was honest and that the change was correct. The most successful individuals and companies in America are those with reputations of high integrity among everyone they deal with. This level of integrity builds the confidence that others have in them and enables them to do more business than their competitors whose ethics may be a little shaky. Earl Nightingale once wrote, "If honesty did not exist, it would have to be invented, as it is the surest way of getting rich." A study at Harvard University concluded that the most valuable asset that a company has is how it is known to its customers, its reputation.

By the same token, your greatest personal asset is the way that you are known to your customers. It is your personal reputation for keeping your word and fulfilling your commitments. Your integrity precedes you and affects all of your interactions with other people. There are several things you can do to move you more rapidly toward becoming the kind of person that you know you are capable of becoming. The first, as I mentioned, is to decide upon your five most important values in life. Organize them in order of priority. Then write a brief paragraph defining what each of those values means to you. A value combined with a definition becomes an organizing principle, a statement that you can use to help you make better decisions. It is a measure and standard which enables you to know how closely you are adhering to your innermost beliefs and convictions.

The second step to developing integrity and character in yourself is to study men and women of great character. Study the lives and stories of people like George Washington, Abraham Lincoln, Winston Churchill, Florence Nightingale, Susan B.

Anthony and Margaret Thatcher. Study the people whose strength of character enabled them to change their world. As you read, think about how they would behave if they were facing the difficulties that you face.

Napoleon Hill, in his book, *The Master Key to Riches,* tells about how he created an imaginary board of personal advisors made up of great figures of history. He chose people like Napoleon, Lincoln, Jesus, and Alexander the Great. Whenever he had to make a decision, he would relax deeply and then imagine that the members of his advisory council were sitting at a large table in front of him. He would then ask them what he should do to deal effectively with a particular situation. In time, they would begin to give him answers, observations, and insights that helped him see more clearly and act more effectively.

You can do the same thing. Select someone that you very much admire for their qualities of courage, tenacity, honesty, or wisdom. Ask yourself, "What would Jesus do in my situation?" or, "What would Lincoln do if he were here at this time?" You will find yourself with guidance that enables you to be the very best person that you can possibly be.

The third and most important step in building your integrity has to do with formulating your approach based on the psychology of human behavior. We know that if you feel a particular way, you will act in a manner consistent with that feeling. For example, if you feel happy, you will act happy. If you feel angry, you will act angry. If you feel courageous, you will act courageously.

But we also know that you don't always start off feeling the way you want to. However, because of the Law of Reversibility, if you act as if you had a particular feeling, the action will generate the feeling consistent with it. You can, in effect, act your way into feeling. You can "fake it until you make it."

You can become a superior human being by consciously acting exactly as the kind of person that you would most like to become. If you behave like an individual of integrity, courage, resolution, persistence and character, you will soon create within yourself the mental structure and habits of such a person. Your actions will become your reality. You will create a personality that is consistent with your highest aspirations.

The more you walk, talk, and behave consistent with your highest values, the more you will like yourself and the better you will feel about yourself. Your self-image will improve and your level of self-acceptance will go up. You will feel stronger, bolder, and more capable of facing any challenge.

There are three primary areas of your life where acting with integrity is crucial. These are the three areas of greatest temptation for forsaking your integrity, as well as the areas of greatest opportunity for building your integrity. When you listen to your inner voice and do what you know to be the right thing in each of these areas, you will have a sense of peace and satisfaction that will lead you on to success and high achievement.

The first area of integrity has to do with your relationships with your family and your friends, the people close to you. Being true to yourself means living in truth with each person in your life. It means refusing to say or do something that you don't believe is right. Living in truth with other people means that you refuse to stay in any situation where you are unhappy with the behavior of another person. You refuse to tolerate it. You refuse to compromise. Psychologists have determined that most stress and negativity comes from attempting to live in a way that is not congruent with your highest values. It is when your life is out of alignment, when you are doing and saying one thing on the outside, but really feeling and believing something different on the inside, that you feel most unhappy. When you decide to become an individual of character and integrity, your first action will be to neutralize or remove all difficult relationships from your life.

This doesn't mean that you have to go and hit somebody over the head with a stick. It simply means that you honestly confront another person and tell them that you are not happy. Tell them that you would like to reorganize this relationship so that you feel more content and satisfied. If the other person is not willing to make adjustments so that you can be happy, it should be clear to you that you don't want to be in this relationship much longer anyway. The second area of integrity has to do with your attitude and behavior toward money. Casualness toward money brings casualties in your financial life. You must be fastidious about your treatment of money, especially other people's money. You must guard your credit rating the same way you would guard your honor. You must pay your bills punctually, or even early. You must keep your promises with regard to your financial commitments.

The third area of integrity has to do with your commitments to others, especially in your business, your work and your sales activities. Always keep your word. Be a man or a woman of honour. If you say that you will do something, do it. If you make a promise, keep it. If you make a commitment, fulfill it. Be known as the kind of person that can be trusted absolutely, no matter what the circumstances.

Your integrity is manifested in your willingness to adhere to the values you hold most dear. It's easy to make promises and hard to keep them, but if you do, every single act of integrity will make your character a little stronger. And as you improve the quality and strength of your character, every other part of your life will improve as well.

49

Continuous Learning

Throughout the developed world, we have moved from an era of manpower to an era of mind power. We have moved from the use of physical muscles to the use of mental muscles. Today the chief sources of value in our society are knowledge and the ability to apply that knowledge in a timely fashion. In the information age, knowledge is king, and those people who develop the ability to continuously acquire new and better forms of knowledge that they can apply to their work and to their lives will be the movers and shakers in our society for the indefinite future.

When you learn and practice the techniques for rapid learning, when you join the learning revolution, you will learn how to unlock the incredible powers of your mind. You will learn how to become smarter and faster than ever before. You will learn how to become a master of your fate rather than being a victim of circumstances. You will learn how to take complete control of your present and future destiny so that you can accomplish and achieve anything you want in life.

Knowledge is doubling every two to three years in almost every occupation and profession, including yours. This means that your knowledge must double every two to three years for you to just stay even. People who are not aggressively and continuously upgrading their knowledge and skills are not staying in the same place. They are falling behind. You see this demonstrated all over the place with massive lay-offs, declining wages, and growing insecurity in the workforce. You see it in the increasing bewilderment and despair on the part of people who are being displaced from low-skill jobs which have either moved overseas or disappeared altogether. We are in the midst of a societal revolution where unionized industrial workers are becoming a smaller and smaller percentage of our workforce each year.

As recently as the 50s and 60s it was common to believe that you finished your schooling, got a job with a large company and stayed with that company for the rest of your life. This was based on the old paradigm of learning. In this old paradigm, life was divided into three parts. First were your "learning" years, during which you got your education, however extensive or limited. Then came your "earning" years. This was the period of time during which you worked for a living. After that came your "yearning" years. This was the period of retirement which would be paid for by social security, savings, and pensions.

Today, with workforce requirements changing so rapidly, you must continually be asking yourself, "What is my next job going to be?" You must also be asking yourself, on a regular basis, "What is my next career going to be?"

Imagine for a moment that your entire company or industry vanished overnight and you had to start all over again in an entirely new business doing an entirely different job. What would it be? And don't think this question is speculative or that it applies to someone else. It is a question that you will probably have to deal with, perhaps far sooner than you expect. In thinking about your new job and your new career, here is the most important question of all: "What do I have to be absolutely, positively excellent at doing, in order to earn an excellent living in my new job and my new career?"

The answer to almost every question and the solution to almost every problem in the world of work is to learn and practice something new and different. When you learn how to use the incredible power of your brain to absorb and apply new ideas and information, you will be able to lead the field and rise to the top of any profession or occupation.

Here's another question for you: What is your most valuable asset? In terms of cash flow, what is the most valuable thing you have? Well, unless you are very rich, or have a family trust account, your most valuable asset is your "earning ability." It is your ability to earn money. It is your ability to apply your knowledge and skill in a timely fashion to get results for which others will pay.

All your education, knowledge, experience, reading, training, and work has contributed toward building up your earning ability. According to the research, the so-called "rich" in America, and in other countries, are almost invariably people who started from common beginnings, often with great disadvantages, and then overcame those circumstances by investing an enormous amount of time and effort on developing their earning ability. And you can do the same thing, starting today, or at any time.

Management consultant Peter Drucker says that the truly educated person today is a person who has learned how to learn continuously throughout life. Tom Peters says that continuous learning may be the only real source of sustainable competitive advantage for individuals and corporations. And Peter Senge, who wrote The Fifth Dimension, says that only learning organizations, those organizations that are capable of taking in new information, adapting it, and using it faster than their competitors, will survive in the fast-changing, competitive world of tomorrow.

The more you know, the better you will be at solving problems and getting results for which people will pay you. The more you know, the more freedom and opportunity you have. And the more you learn and the faster you learn it, the more rapidly you move upward and onward in your career and in every other area of your life.

Between where you are and where you want to go, there is almost always a gap, and in almost every case you will find that you can bridge this gap with knowledge and skills. In order to get from where you are to your goals, you have to learn and practice something new and different. You have to learn new skills and abilities. You have to learn new attitudes and methods. You have to learn new techniques and practices. If you want to be a better parent, you must learn and practice better parenting skills. If you want to be a better spouse, you must study and practice relationship skills. If you want to earn more money, you have to determine what it is that people will pay more money for, and then get busy learning and practicing those behaviors.

Specific knowledge and specific skills will become obsolete with the passing of time, but learning how to learn is a permanent skill that you can use all the days of your life. The people who join the learning revolution, and who learn how to learn faster, like those people who first learned how to operate computers, or learned how to become excellent in their fields, will be able to earn more in one or two years of work than the average person earns in perhaps five or ten years.

By joining the learning revolution, you will enhance every area of your life. You will be able to help your spouse and your children unlock and realize more of their individual potentials. You will be a better friend in helping your friends use more of their abilities. And you will be a better manager, developing the skills that will enable you to get far more out of yourself and other people than ever before.